Annegret Oehme
**"He should have listened to his wife!"**

Annegret Oehme

# "He should have listened to his wife!"

The Construction of Women's Roles in German and Yiddish Pre-modern *Wigalois* Adaptations

DE GRUYTER

ISBN 978-3-11-062199-0
e-ISBN (PDF) 978-3-11-062440-3
e-ISBN (EPUB) 978-3-11-067836-9

**Library of Congress Control Number: 2019949185**

**Bibliographic information published by the Deutsche Nationalbibliothek**
The Deutsche Nationalbibliothek lists this publication in the Deutsche Nationalbibliografie;
detailed bibliographic data are available on the Internet at http://dnb.dnb.de.

© 2020 Walter de Gruyter GmbH, Berlin/Boston
Cover image: A poor woman drags the unconscious Wigalois to the river (vv. 5383-5453), Wirnt
von Grafenberg, Wigalois, Cistercian convent of Amelungsborn, 1372. Leiden University Library,
LTK 537, fol. 57v. Photo: Leiden University Library.
Printing and binding: CPI books GmbH, Leck

www.degruyter.com

For Andrea and Flurina

# Acknowledgements

The idea of this book goes back to Kathryn Starkey's graduate seminar on Arthurian literature. The topic of Wigalois proved so interesting that it led to several projects, of which this book represents one. My deep gratitude goes to Kathryn Starkey and Ann Marie Rasmussen who provided feedback along the way, and most of all to my tireless former "Doktormutter" Ruth von Bernuth who not only offered academic guidance to the then graduate student, but also found time to discuss the intricacies of Early New High German spelling issues with the now junior faculty living almost a continent away.

I am very grateful to my wonderful colleagues and office neighbors Kye Terrasi and Jason Groves for their constant encouragement and high spirits, and Ellwood Wiggins for the help with some translations.

I am truly grateful to the anonymous reviewers of this manuscript who presented peer-review at its best: precise in their feedback and constructive in their criticism.

My greatest thanks go to Jesús, constant and tireless motivator and coach, concerned nutritionist, and partner in crime.

It seems poetic justice that I finished the manuscript corrections in North Carolina, where all of this began.

# Contents

| | | |
|---|---|---|
| 1 | **Introduction** —— 1 | |
| 1.1 | Adapting Arthur: The Wigalois Tradition —— 5 | |
| 1.2 | Beyond the Canon: Researching the *Wigalois* Adaptations —— 8 | |
| | | |
| 2 | ***Wigalois:* Exalting Female Devotion** —— 13 | |
| 2.1 | Female Figures between Provision and Devotion —— 15 | |
| 2.2 | "Against Her Will": Sexual Violence Against Women in *Wigalois* —— 20 | |
| 2.3 | Wild Women: *Wigalois'* Transgressive Women —— 25 | |
| 2.4 | Conclusion —— 31 | |
| | | |
| 3 | ***Wigoleis:* Mother Mary's Maidens** —— 33 | |
| 3.1 | Mary's Divine Presence in *Wigoleis* —— 35 | |
| 3.2 | Female Victimhood and Transgression —— 41 | |
| 3.3 | Aesthetics of Passivity —— 46 | |
| 3.4 | Conclusion —— 50 | |
| | | |
| 4 | ***Viduvilt:* Mothers Seizing Power** —— 52 | |
| 4.1 | From Patriarchy to Matriarchy: Viduvilt's Name and Heritage —— 56 | |
| 4.2 | Family Politics —— 58 | |
| 4.3 | Neither Lilith nor Eve: Revisiting Misogynist Role Models —— 61 | |
| 4.4 | Conclusion —— 65 | |
| | | |
| 5 | **Epilogue** —— 68 | |

**Bibliography** —— 71

# 1 Introduction

In the winter of 2017, I taught a class on Arthurian Romances. I included a broad variety of canonized as well as non-traditional material, such as the Middle High German romance *Wigalois* (1210/1220) by Wirnt von Grafenberg and *Viduvilt*, an early modern anonymous Yiddish adaptation of Wirnt's romance (sixteenth century). The class began with the 2004 movie *King Arthur*, in which a dying Lancelot provides Guinevere with the reassurance that their stories will not be forgotten: "And as for the knights who gave their lives, their deaths were cause for neither mourning nor sadness. For they will live forever, their names and deeds handed down from father to son, mother to daughter, in the legends of King Arthur and his knights" (*King Arthur* 2004). With these words, Lancelot reflects on how he and the other Knights of the Round Table will live on through stories. In the process of adaptation, cause and effect become interchangeable. The movie anticipates how the events narrated over the past two hours reinforce well-known stories about King Arthur and his knights, stories about men. Guinevere should not be comforted by these words; contemporary movies such as *King Arthur* focus on the Arthurian story world as that of men.

The students felt both intrigued and disturbed by the portrayal of women in this movie, which features Guinevere (Keira Knightley) on the battlefield wearing a two-piece outfit that displays much more than it conceals and seems the least practical combat outfit imaginable. Taken aback by such imagery, one of my students proposed an honors project: to analyze the presentation of Guinevere in six popular Arthurian movies with which many students were familiar, all made between 1953 and 2004. In order to analyze the portrayal of Guinevere as the most prominent woman in the movies, the student used both the Bechdel Test and the so-called Sexy Lamp Test. The Bechdel test, popularized by the American cartoonist Alison Bechdel, focuses on three questions: (1) Does the movie have at least two (named) women in it? (2) do these women talk with each other? (3) do they talk about anything besides men? The so-called Sexy Lamp Test draws on a prominent object in *A Christmas Story* (1983), a lamp that features a lampshade over a fake leg in a black pump, dressed in a fishnet stocking. As a supplement to the Bechdel Test, this approach asks whether the story would be affected if a female character were to be removed and replaced with the lamp from *A Christmas Story*. The results were disillusioning albeit not surprising. None of the six Arthurian movies passed the Bechdel test and only two passed the Sexy Lamp Test. Guinevere is only named in three movies, despite being clearly identifiable as King Arthur's female love interest. She is saved by a man at some point in each movie and is portrayed as (at least potentially) an adulterer every time[1], subsequently becoming a nun in three out of six films. The containment of women's (sexual) power, the emphasis on their lust as well as their dependence on and need to be "saved" by men, connects all the films my student reviewed. Not surprisingly, none of these films features a single woman writer, director, or producer. My students, aware of alternative narratives from the class material, were incredibly frustrated by these mainstream Hollywood interpretations. The movies, my students concluded, were more "medieval" than the medieval material itself. More recent movies do not change this impression significantly. The second time I taught the Arthurian class, I replaced *King Arthur* with *King Arthur: Legend of the Sword* (*King Arthur* 2017), another father-son story, a "bromance" that seems to suggest that the Arthurian story world is a universe without diverse female roles and most certainly without powerful women.

As part of a larger and still ongoing adaptation tradition revolving around King Arthur and his Knights of the Round Table, the Wigalois material offers a fascinating case study through which one can critically revisit the portrayal of women's roles in the Arthurian canon. Women are central to a knight's success in medieval Arthurian romantic literature. However, as Maureen Fries has documented, even the verbs chosen to describe women's actions in such texts tend to cast women's roles as passive, in contrast to their active male counterparts (Fries 1996, 61–63). And even when women are granted significant agency, "women's power" is a narrative fiction that centers male subjectivity, as Roberta Krueger has shown: the hero needs the woman to resist so that he can desire her (Krueger 1996, 242). Yet the role of women in Arthurian literature is constantly negotiated and reformulated—it is indeed complicated (Burns 2013, 403). Middle High German (MHG) literature even includes an entire genre focused on powerful and active female figures: women's epic, a genre classification established by Inga Wild in the 1970s (and subsequently used by Jerold Frakes) that includes such works as *Nibelungenlied*, *Klage,* and *Kudrun*. Even in traditional Arthurian narratives, women are not necessarily just powerless extras on a knight's path to success. In one well-known example, the noble lady Enite, from Hartmann von Aue's MHG *Erec* adaptation (1180/1190) repeatedly saves the Arthurian knight Erec against his explicit wishes, but thereby ensures both his success as a knight and the liberation of eighty mourning widows. The grotesque but all-wise Cundrie, the messenger maiden of the grail who sets straight the young and very

---

[1] In *King Arthur* (2004), an affair between Lancelot and Guinevere is never explicit, but a few sequences hint at a possible relationship between the two with more scenes between the two included in the director's cut of the film.

naïve would-be knight Parzival in Wolfram von Eschenbach's MHG *Parzival* (1200/1210) represents another. While vastly different, they both represent female figures evaluated generally in a positive light. Nevertheless, their overstepping of boundaries ultimately serves each text's hero. These contradictions and complexities require further exploration, as Jane Burns points out: "the tensions, questions, and debates about gendered identities [are] posed by a system that challenges and critiques courtly traditions even as it enacts them." (2013, 408).

In this monograph, I move beyond a simple agency/no-agency dichotomy; instead, I explore the construction of female figures and the consequences for their respective adaptations, in regard to both the text itself and the contemporaneous reception of the text. Overlooking the construction of female figures simply because they support the knights, however, wrongly simplifies the female figures' complicated depictions and unintentionally reinforces a stronger scholarly interest in male characters (Fenster 1996, xli). Furthermore, this dismissive approach has led scholars to neglect the border-crossing power of female devotion in *Wigalois*, as I will show in my first chapter.

To demonstrate the subtlety and complexity of women's portrayals in medieval Arthurian romances, I explore the representation of female figures in three texts of the Wigalois universe: Wirnt von Grafenberg's *Wigalois* (1210/1220), the earliest medieval representative and point of comparison for the other two texts; and two early modern, anonymously-authored adaptations: the Early New High German *Wigoleis vom Rade* [*Wigoleis of the Wheel*] (1483/1493 and 1519), and the Old Yiddish *Viduvilt* (sixteenth century). *Wigalois* best embodies the complicated relationship of Arthurian romances with the portrayal of female figures. Just as other contemporaneous literary texts *Wigalois* at points presents its audience with misogynist commentaries on women while also offering a positive take on an essentially gendered topic of devotion that connects all women and even crosses religious-cultural borders. Defying a simple modern "progressive" or "conservative" evaluation even more, *Wigalois* includes a wide spectrum of female figures (most of them named) beyond the stereotypical courtly damsel in distress: a confident messenger maiden, a wild woman in the woods, and a bellicose Amazon, to name only a few. Within the broad spectrum of female figures, several of them have significant agency at some point but are eventually subordinated to serving the knight. This feature is not singular to *Wigalois*. In this chapter, I focus on the inherent contradictions of the portrayal of female figures within the MHG romance, contradictions that two early modern adaptations tried to solve by taking the narrative in very different directions.

The second text examined in this monograph, *Wigoleis*, addresses the complex and contradictory depiction of women by reinforcing the ideal of passive women found in *Wigalois*. Within that context, it uniquely transposes the unifying feature of devotion through an inspirational role model, particularly for its female audience, by incorporating a religious figure: Mary, mother of Jesus. Since this adaptation is directly tied to the woodcuts that popularized it, this discussion will approach the narrative's visual as well as discursive elements. The third text discussed here, the Yiddish *Viduvilt*, shows that the Wigalois narrative universe need not inherently require the restriction of female figures, but rather that very different portrayals of women coexist in contemporaneous adaptations. *Viduvilt* focuses on *Wigalois*' strong female figures and expands their agency so much that it ultimately offers a radical new interpretation of the narrative, displaying a drastic power shift towards a matriarchal story world.

The example of *Viduvilt* underscores that the construction of female figures has everything to do with their relative access to agency. Agency can be defined as "ability or capacity to act or exert power".[2] Figures who lack agency occupy the position of object rather than subject; they are acted upon or instrumentalized to the development of more active characters rather than acting in their own right. Having agency, by contrast, places characters in a position of power over their own fate as well as the fates of others. I examine the construction of female figures with a particular focus on agency across these texts as means of comparison, first, to understand each text's respective contributions to the Wigalois and larger Arthurian literary tradition; second, to make sense of how each text interacts with its predecessors; and third, to explore how they prepare the path for later adaptations. Since changes in gender representation reveal new connections across *Wigalois* adaptations, this study contributes a long overdue analysis of core Arthurian texts to Adaptation Studies. I use the term "adaptation" in accordance with Linda Hutcheon, who emphasizes the special value of adaptations by emphasizing their triple identity as formal units or products, as acts of (re)creation, and as acts of reception (Hutcheon 2006, 111). In the case of the portrayal of female figures in the Wigalois material, we will see that the representation of women allows us to perceive *Viduvilt* and *Wigoleis* through Adaptation Studies' sense of triple identity as the adaptors address the contradictions inherent in *Wigalois* while simultaneously creating their own entry into the tradition that does not require familiarity with preceding material.

Historically, the Wigalois tradition has been perceived within a stark Christian-Jewish divide. Scholarship on the "Jewish character" of the Yiddish often concentrates on women figures behaving in a "Jewish manner," or on the text's representation of famous Jewish mythical figures such as Lilith, the supposed first wife of Adam (Jaeger 2000; Warnock 1981). This scholarly focus

---

[2] See "agency, n." (*OED Online*).

stands in contrast to the little attention female characters from the German *Wigalois* and *Wigoleis* have received. I evaluate these three texts not as Christian or Jewish but as Arthurian, showing that the construction of female figures – separate from their religious associations – allows for a new and meaningful approach to all three adaptations.

## 1.1 Adapting Arthur: The Wigalois Tradition

The myth of King Arthur is conspicuous in literary history, having prompted one of the most productive adaptation traditions throughout Europe and beyond. Within this framework, the Wigalois material is as representative of the general Arthurian tradition as it is exceptional. It is representative because the retellings include different versions in media, textual representation, and genre. It is exceptional because the adaptations involve two seemingly distinct linguistic and cultural groups, Jewish Yiddish-speaking and the Christian German-speaking audiences, and yet culminate in one shared narrative tradition.

Wirnt's MHG romance[3] was itself a product of a transcultural and translingual narrative network, potentially sharing a textual source with the Old French *Le Bel Inconnu* (c. 1191–1213) by Renaut de Beaujeu. *Wigalois* rather traditionally focuses on a knight's rite of passage, in which the errant knight completes a series of quests in order to obtain land and wife, kingdom and vassals. Scholars have generally agreed with the proposition that Wirnt's *Wigalois* portrays the tale of an exemplary knight, one whose path is free from true crises.[4] As the son of the (mostly) exemplary knight Gawein, Wigalois seems to conform to the family tradition. The narrative as portrayed in *Wigalois* begins with the protagonist's parentage: Gawein is led from King Arthur's court to a mysterious, faraway land and marries its princess. After a period of time, however, Gawein returns to the Arthurian court, unaware of his wife's pregnancy. Years later, Wigalois, now an adult, travels to the Arthurian court himself in search of his father. Once there, he is challenged with a quest, which in turn leads to a series of ad-

---

[3] Despite Wigalois not being featured in other Arthurian romances, he is, however, mentioned in the MHG *Kudrun:* "When Hilde and her daughter entered the hall in front of Wigalois' house, they heard a loud noise [...]." ["Dô Hilde und ihr tohter / giengen in den sal, vor Wigâleises hûse / sie hôrten dicke schal [...]."] (*Kudrun*, 582). This reference interestingly indicates a crossover from the Arthurian realm into heroic epic.
[4] See for example Brinker-von der Heyde 1995, 94; Fasbender 2010, 86; Fuchs 1997, 120; Grubmüller 1985, 224; Heinzle 1973, 267; Lichtblau 2011, 221; Thomas 2005, 70. Several scholars, however, oppose this common interpretation (Eming 1999, 144; Lohbeck 1991, 289–290).

ventures. Eventually, he accomplishes his primary task, freeing a besieged kingdom from its "heathen" usurper.[5] As a reward, Wigalois then marries the princess of the formerly bewitched land and becomes its new king. Following these events, a significant part of the remaining narrative covers an epic battle that draws on the tradition of the *chanson de geste*, a type of story centered on the Christian-heathen wars associated with Charlemagne. Most of the adaptations, however, do not include this extensive epic battle. Thus, in contrast to *Wigalois*, later adaptations present a more typical Arthurian romance in the narratological tradition of the Arthurian romances of the MHG author Hartmann von Aue or of his inspiration, Chrétien de Troyes.

Wirnt's *Wigalois*, the first German example of this fairly obscure narrative tradition, proved to be widely successful, not only with its intended thirteenth-century audiences. More than 28 fragments and 13 complete manuscripts of *Wigalois* still exist, with the earliest dating from 1220–1230, shortly after its composition (Wennerhold 2005, 76–77, 80). Moreover, within the span of several hundred years, the story was reworked into Early New High German prose at least three times, once as a stand-alone text, *Wigoleis vom Rade*, and twice as an interpolated text within larger romance compilations, namely Ulrich Füetrer's Early New High German *Buch der Abenteuer* [*Book of Adventures*] (1473–1487)[6] and Sigmund Feyerabend's Early New High German *Buch der Liebe* [*Book of Love*] (1587).[7] In the 1390s, the Wigalois material was also adapted in an exclusively visual form as a mural cycle at Castle Runkelstein (Roncolo) in South Tyrol.

The Old Yiddish adaptation, commonly referred to as *Viduvilt*, also highlights this broad historical reception of *Wigalois*. The Yiddish text represents the first known rendering of an Arthurian text in this language.[8] Unfortunately,

---

**5** I keep the texts' terminology "heathen" as it is not the same as Muslims or Islam but rather presents a group of others as worshipers of a polytheist but largely undefined cult that evokes powers of Roman gods as well as Muhammad, and sometimes even Satan. The presentation of the "heathens" aims at presenting a culturally weak group and brand members as not belonging to Christianity and as a consequence not having access to salvation (see also Lembke 2017, 24; Frakes 2011, 33).
**6** See "Wigoleis." *Buch der Abenteuer der Ritter von der Tafelrunde*, ed. Ulrich Füetrer (1473–1487), Bayerische Staatsbibliothek, CGM 1, 75 r.–83r.
**7** "Ritterliche History des Hochberühmpten und Thewren Ritters Herrn Wigoleis vom Rade...." See *Buch der Liebe*. ed. Sigmund Feyerabend. Frankfurt, 1587. 382–396.
**8** The diaspora culture of the Jews in the Holy Roman Empire might not come to mind as a potential participant in the retellings of Arthurian stories. However, and in addition to the Yiddish *Wigalois* adaptations, it produced at least one Hebrew-language Arthurian adaptation [*Melekh Artus*] ("King Arthur") from 1279, loosely based on sections from the Old French *Lancelot-*

authorship, date, and place of composition remain unknown. The preserved sixteenth-century manuscripts point to Italy as the place of composition; during the period, Italy was a central location for the production of Yiddish literature (Dreeßen 1994, 85; Jaeger 2000, 29), while later adaptations appear to have come from further north. Although only three incomplete manuscripts of this first Yiddish adaptation are preserved, *Viduvilt* became a template for numerous reworkings, including *Sir Gabein* (1789), an adaptation in which the main character travels to China and Russia, and becomes heir to the Chinese imperial throne. This fascination with *Viduvilt* among Yiddish-speaking audiences lasted for centuries. The most famous reworking of the text, *Artis Hof* (printed in Amsterdam in 1671), is about 1,000 lines longer than the first Yiddish adaptation.

The Yiddish adaptations bridged the seventeenth-century gap, a time in which the stories of King Arthur were not reworked within the German-speaking world. Even though Arthurian stories enjoyed immense popularity in this area during the Middle Ages, they fell into oblivion, only to be rediscovered near the end of the eighteenth century (which was also the case, interestingly, for the German "national" epic, the *Nibelungenlied*).[9] In a German translation of Erasmus of Rotterdam's *Moriae Encomium (In Praise of Folly)* from 1780, Arthurian narrative was sufficiently obscure that the translator added a footnote explaining to his German audience who King Arthur was: "Arthur was one of the oldest kings of England, who defended himself against the Anglo-Saxons."[10] But the Yiddish story of the Arthurian knight Wigalois continued to be retold, mediated by the Protestant philosopher and Hebraist Johann Christoph Wagenseil, who transliterated, translated and reprinted *Artis Hof* [*Arthur's Court*] (1671/ 1679) in his Yiddish textbook for non-Jews, *Belehrung der Jüdisch-Teutschen Red- und Schreibart* [*Introduction to Spoken and Written Jewish-German*] (1699), thereby making the adaptation accessible to a non-Yiddish speaking audience.[11] Wagenseil himself includes a short introductory comment concerning Arthur, in which he displays neither a love for the English people nor an anticipated audience's familiarity with Arthurian tales. In 1780, Daniel Ernst Wagner reworked Wagenseil's version for his collection of narratives entitled *Erzehlungen aus*

---

*Grail* prose cycle. About the Hebrew Arthurian romance, see further Leviant 1969; Rovang 2009, 3–9; and Przybilski 2002, 409–435.
**9** It is, however, important to note that this was not the case in the English-speaking world, where the Arthurian tradition continued uninterruptedly. For a further discussion on the "return" of the Arthurian material in the German-speaking context, see Oergel 1998.
**10** "Arthur war einer der ältesten Könige von England, der sich wider die Angelsachsen vertheidigte." (Erasmus von Rotterdam 1780, 281).
**11** See Wagenseil 1699.

*dem Heldenalter teutscher Nationen* [*Tales from the German Nations' Heroic Age*], using the story to evoke a spirit of "Germanness" that he suggested dated back to the Middle Ages.¹² Around the same time, Johann Ferdinand Roth produced an alternative retelling in his *Vom Könige Artus und von dem bildschönen Ritter Wieduwilt. Ein Ammenmährchen* [*About King Arthur and the beautiful Sir Wieduwilt. An Old Wives' Tale*] (1786). While title and introduction point to Wagenseil as the source of inspiration, Roth offers his own take on the narrative, using it to create a sort of anti-Catholic genre parody. Even the famous German romantic poet Ludwig Uhland (1787–1862) drew on the transliterated Yiddish version rather than the German tradition for a fragmentary poem he composed titled "Ritter Wieduwilt".¹³ In all these instances, it is noteworthy that the eighteenth- and nineteenth-century adaptors did not refer to the Middle High German or later German versions, but rather reworked a story that was itself a product of different European traditions transmitted through the Yiddish versions that "saved" King Arthur from oblivion in the German-speaking context.

In recent years, the Wigalois narrative has seen a series of new adaptations as a result of the enthusiastic work of the *Kulturverein Wirnt von Gräfenberg e.V.* [Cultural Association Wirnt von Gräfenberg, Non-Profit Organization], an institution based in Gräfenberg, Franconia, the medieval poet's presumptive hometown. The organization's mission is to preserve and create new interest in the work of Wirnt von Grafenberg. Under the leadership of the group's initiator, Manfred Schwab, the group produced a graphic novel in 2011, a play in 2012, and a children's opera in 2014.¹⁴

## 1.2 Beyond the Canon: Researching the *Wigalois* Adaptations

Despite a successful 800-year adaptation tradition, Wirnt von Grafenberg's *Wigalois* was devalued in nineteenth- and twentieth-century scholarship as a "postclassical" Arthurian romance, marred by an eclectic use of derivative material.¹⁵ This changed only in recent decades. Attempting either to deconstruct the value of *Wigalois* as courtly Arthurian romance or to demonstrate Wirnt's genius with his original take on the established Arthurian tradition, scholars compared *Wigalois* to romances by the "classical" MHG poet Hartmann von Aue or to Wolfram

---

12 See "Wieduwilt," 1780, 382–517.
13 See Uhland 1898, 159–161.
14 See Bartoll, Monés, and Schwab 2011.
15 Scholars such as Werner Schröder have been particularly critical of the excessive use of magic and mystical elements in Wirnt's contribution to this tradition (Schröder 1986, 235–277).

von Eschenbach's *Parzival*, itself a bold adaptation of Chrétien de Troyes' Old French *Perceval* (fragment, 1180/90). At stake in these comparisons was the scholarly value of the *Wigalois* romance and its classification as canonical or non-canonical. Perhaps as a consequence, *Wigalois* did not receive broad attention in an academic context and in university literature courses until fairly recently. Despite the initial lack of scholarly interest, research and publications on *Wigalois* have increased immensely during the last two decades.[16] The increase in research has led to several new translations, including an excellent modern German translation based on the 1926 Kapteyn facing-page edition of *Wigalois* with extensive commentary by Sabine and Ulrich Seelbach (published in 2005, 2nd ed. 2014),[17] Danielle Buschinger's French *Wigalois, le chevalier à la roue* (2004), and an English translation by J. W. Thomas (1977).[18] Recent research covers a range of topics, including descriptive analyses of newly found fragments, the question of the hero's messianism, and gender construction.[19] German monographs that discuss *Wigalois* in context with other contemporaneous works include Amelie Bendheim's 2017 *Wechselrahmen: Medienhistorische Fallstudien zum Romananfang des 13. Jahrhunderts* (*Flore und Blanscheflur, Wigalois, Wigamur*). In conversation with Bendheim, Pia Selmayr discusses the construction of the Otherworld in *Wigalois* in connection with *Lanzelet*, another contemporaneous MHG text, concluding that the essential function of this world lies in illuminating and reframing the universe of the court (Selmayr 2018). By building on Selmayr's argument with regard to the "wild woman," one of the most prominent otherworldly characters within Wigalois narratives, I examine this character's diverse representations across the three different adaptations.

Similar to the MHG *Wigalois*, the Yiddish adaptations are slowly being discovered by a broader scholarly audience for two important reasons. First, translations and new editions are making the Old Yiddish texts known and accessible to a broader audience.[20] Since both *Viduvilt* and *Wigalois* are available as English

---

**16** The *Bibliographie der Deutschen Sprach- und Literaturwissenschaft* alone lists 68 publications on *Wigalois* from the last ten years.
**17** See Wirnt von Grafenberg 2014; Wirnt von Grafenberg 1926.
**18** See Wirnt von Grafenberg 2004; Wirnt von Grafenberg 1977. Joseph M. Sullivan is currently preparing a facing-page Middle High German edition with modern English translation that will appear in the Boydell and Brewer "Arthurian Archives" series, expected in 2021. This edition will be completely new, based on the Leiden Manuscript B.
**19** Examples include Bertelsmeier-Kierst 2015, 150–177; Böcking 2013, 363–380; and Fasbender, 2013, 209–222.
**20** For the English-speaking world, Jerold Frakes has undertaken the enormous effort to make a large amount of Old Yiddish material accessible through translations and scholarly guides. Also, a recent new edition of the *Bove Bukh* by Claudia Rosenzweig offers new and critical access to a

translations, an audience familiar with these texts need not speak German. Second, contemporary historians, such as Verena Kasper-Marienberg and Jonathan Elukin, are revisiting the assumption that the Jewish Yiddish-speaking minority in the Holy Roman Empire led an existence separate from the Christian, German-speaking majority and had little or no impact on the latter's culture. Largely using primary sources, these historians are uncovering an intricate network of cultural interaction and cross-fertilization. Significantly, recent research on Old Yiddish[21] literature supports these historical claims, revealing a more intimate form of cultural mixing than court documents or commercial exchanges alone would convey – namely, the one told through stories. Comparative interpretations of different adaptations from within this multilingual and intercultural narrative tradition have emerged from this increase in research on *Wigalois* and *Viduvilt*.

My project situates the adaptations in relation to each other without prioritizing *Wigalois*. Rather than merely assigning the respective text a Jewish or Christian identity (and, hence, addressed to two presumably separate and disconnected audiences), this comparative examination of women and agency across Wigalois narratives furthers an understanding of both diachronic and synchronic changes in the adaptations. Overcoming the Yiddish-German separation and highlighting an adaption studies approach, my work is inherently comparative. I believe that this close analysis of *Wigoleis* and *Viduvilt* as early modern reactions to *Wigalois* allows us to move beyond simplified judgements of the material.

My approach is built upon several studies that brought adaptations in other constellations into a dialogue. Achim Jaeger's 2000 monograph *Ein jüdischer Artusritter* (*Wigalois*, *Viduvilt*) particularly emphasizes the value of comparative studies of these texts. His detailed analysis of the Old Yiddish retelling had a significant impact on the revaluation of the *Wigalois* adaptations in general. Any critical examination of *Viduvilt* and its scholarship, such as Jaeger's thesis of the "Jewish Arthurian knight" which I will problematize later, is in the first place only possible thanks to his pioneering and extensive work on *Viduvilt*. Further examples of comparative analysis include Astrid Lembke's "Ritter außer Gefecht" (*Wigalois*, *Viduvilt*), which discusses the construction of the hero's identity

---

classic of Old Yiddish (Bovo d'Antona by Elye Bokher. A Yiddish Romance: A Critical Edition with Commentary. Leiden: Brill, 2016).
**21** The question as to whether or not this early form of Yiddish is a language in its own right or merely a dialect is as contested as the name (Old Yiddish, West-Yiddish, Early Yiddish, Jewish-German, Hebrew-German to name just a few). See among many others Berger 2008, 86; Baumgarten 2005, 1–25; Frakes 1988; Wexler 1988.

in relationship to the women he encounters along the way; Bianca Häberlein's "Transformationen religiöser und profaner Motive" (*Wigalois, Viduvilt, Ammenmährchen*), which focuses on several retellings in the light of changing audiences and modifications based on their respective cultural and religious needs; Wulf-Otto Dreeßen's "Wandlungen des Artusromans im Jiddischen" (*Wigalois, Viduvilt*), a close reading based on the culture behind the Yiddish material; and Jutta Eming's 1999 *Funktionswandel des Wunderbaren* (*Bel Inconnu, Wigalois, Wigoleis vom Rade*), in which she analyzes the texts' marvelous elements in connection with their respective epochal changes in aesthetics. James Brown's 2016 study, *Imagining the Text*, surpasses the prior comparative analyses by combining research on verbal (written stories and also the ones transmitted in the courtly oral context) and pictorial adaptations in order to explain the reception processes undergone to engage with the *Wigalois* adaptations. While Brown emphasizes the cross-fertilization of the pictorial and verbal traditions with a focus only on the German texts, I focus on the topic of agential women, emphasizing another approach to the tradition and highlighting the interconnectedness of Yiddish and German adaptations.

Extending this exploration within the context of Adaptation Studies to include more modern works can benefit readers because it offers insight into modern perceptions of the Middle Ages, highlighting how adaptations are connected and react to each other. An analysis of this material through the lens of adaptations abolishes notions of textual autonomy (Böhme 2007, vii; Hutcheon 2006, 6, 111). Rather than perceiving Wirnt's text as the ultimate entry in this tradition and its successors as mere copies measured against the "original", this approach "democratizes" the material by placing the distinct adaptations into dialogue. Similarly, this framework does not privilege discursive over visual material. Of course, any subsequent encounter with another source is impacted by familiarity with the first adaptation a reader accessed (also Hutcheon 2006, 29). Thomas Leitch (2008, 106) and Jørgen Bruhn have emphasized this dialogical identity of Adaptation Studies: "[We] should study both the source and result of the adaptation as two texts, infinitely changing positions, taking turns being sources for each other in the ongoing work of the reception in the adaptational process." (Bruhn 2013, 73). Post-Wirnt *Wigalois* adaptations have unfortunately been judged as outdated or deficient compared to *Wigalois*. This approach provides an important corrective, enabling contemporary readers to appreciate the adaptations as independently valuable and innovative texts. An audience aware of an artifact's identity as adaptation alternates between two or more works regardless of their diachronic production or supposed scholarly value. Adaptation Studies emphasizes the relationship of a retelling of a story and its model as a dialogue, a two-way process (Bruhn 2013, 74). This brings the process of production and reception closer together, which is important for the Wigalois narratives, where adaptations regularly become models for a new reworking themselves or, at the very least, often reference preceding material. An audience might read an adaptation first and then later compare it to Wirnt's text. In the case of a reader unfamiliar with the Wigalois tradition, the encounter with any post-Wirnt adaptation abolishes dominant ideas of an ideal historic model text.

## 2 *Wigalois:* Exalting Female Devotion

Now, out of the Christian spiritualizing force blossoms the strangest phenomenon of the Middle Ages: knighthood, which is eventually sublimated into spiritual knighthood. The worldly knighthood, we see most gracefully exalted in the legends of King Arthur, in which the sweetest gallantry, the most well-bred *courtoisie*, and the most adventurous combativeness prevail. In the sweet, quixotic arabesques and fantastic floral constructs of those poems we are greeted by the delightful Iwein, the splendid Lanzelot of the Lake, and the brave, gallant, decent, but slightly boring Wigalois.[1]

("Nun aber, aus der christlich spiritualisierten Kraft, entfaltet sich die eigentümlichste Erscheinung des Mittelalters, das Rittertum, das sich endlich noch sublimiert als ein geistliches Rittertum. Jenes, das weltliche Rittertum, sehen wir am anmutigsten verherrlicht in dem Sagenkreis des Königs Artus, worin die süßeste Galanterie, die ausgebildetste *courtoisie* und die abenteuerlichste Kampflust herrscht. Aus den süß närrischen Arabesken und phantastischen Blumengebilden dieser Gedichte grüßen uns der köstliche Iwein, der vortreffliche Lanzelot vom See und der tapfere, galante, honette, aber etwas langweilige Wigalois." Heine 1887, 126)

"Boring." This is the famed German poet Heinrich Heine's humorous assessment of Wirnt von Grafenberg's *Wigalois*. Up to the late twentieth century, Heine (1797–1856) was not alone in his verdict. In fact, until recently, Wirnt's *Wigalois* had not been perceived as the most fascinating representative of its genre. Treating Chrétien de Troyes' and Hartmann von Aue's Arthurian Romances as the "classical" and "ideal," early scholars were primarily interested in the use of magic and religion in Wirnt's text.[2]

In the handwritten original to "Die Romantische Schule," Heine highlights another element of *Wigalois* based on his own impression: "But I firmly believe that the lovely courtly ladies of the Middle Ages enjoyed this reading much more, not least because of the colorful descriptions of clothing with which such poetry perhaps filled the role of modern fashion journal." ("Ich bin aber überzeugt, daß die minniglichen Burgfrauen des Mittelalters sich an dieser Lektüre viel besser erbaut, schon wegen der bunten Kleiderschilderungen, wodurch solche Dichtungen vielleicht die Stelle der modernen Modejournale vertraten." Heine 1887, 157). Women, the poet concludes in his usual ironic tone, must have found the exces-

---

[1] Translations by the author, unless otherwise noted.
[2] This debate continues. In 2016, Helmut Beifuss published his study participating in a central debate about the religious aspect of both the text and the hero (a debate most prominently featured in Stephan Fuchs (1997) *Hybride Helden*). Beifuss reaffirms older arguments that cast *Wigalois* as a more-or-less coherently religious tale with a pious hero who succeeds thanks to divine support.

sive descriptions of clothing particularly entertaining. Heine's association of garments with women represents a connection already established within *Wigalois* albeit with a different emphasis: the women of *Wigalois* provide the hero with armor for the quest or dress the naked hero wandering in the wild woods. Providing clothes and armor directly impacts the Arthurian knight's successful quest.

Some scholars have argued that women in *Wigalois*, compared to their Arthurian predecessors, become the mere "conflict-free" extras for a successful and renowned knight (in particular Böcking 2013, 380; Leidinger 2013, 409). Wolfram von Eschenbach's MHG *Parzival*, the romance with which *Wigalois* is most often compared, introduces its audience to a broad spectrum of female figures, several of them with significant agency. For example, Cundrie, the Grail's messenger maiden, is portrayed as wise and influential despite her outer, grotesque features, at the time an unusual choice. Another contemporary MHG poet, Hartmann von Aue, presents his audience with women who illustrate a complex concept of agency; for instance, Lunete and Laudine (*Iwein*) and Enite (*Erec*) are courtly women of different social status, shown in situations where they have to make decisions consequential for them and the text's main male Arthurian heroes.

Wirnt, however, presents a broader range of female figures than Hartmann, including some as unusual as Wolfram's Cundrie, but ultimately restricts their agency in comparison to the normative female passive figure at the Arthurian court. The central conflicts in *Wigalois* lie in the besieged kingdom of Korntin and in the hero's battle with supernatural forces, not in love and marriage, as is the case in Hartmann's romances *Erec* and *Iwein* or the Gawein story in *Parzival* (Mertens 1981, 23). As a consequence, Wirnt's women are less relevant in the context of love and marriage but are placed in a broader variety of roles, including a combat between Wigalois and the wild woman Ruel.

In this chapter, I explore the array of possible constructions of female figures and how, ultimately, these figures are presented and judged within the text according to a relatively simple schema of normative feminine behavior. At first glance, Wigalois presents its audience with powerless women, female victims who rely on knightly heroes and women who depend so much on a male counterpart that they themselves cease to exist when he vanishes. I discuss these cases, but I also show how Wirnt grapples with the construction of female figures. *Wigalois* presents a surprisingly wide range of female character types, including an Amazon fighting alongside Arthurian knights and a wild woman on a quest to revenge her husband's murder. Wirnt's experiment leads to the portrayal of a broad range of female figures, the inclusion of several women entering into physical fights, and women who support the knightly hero on his way to success. As we will see, however, these active women stepping out of the designated sphere of acceptable activity problematize the narrative's logic and ultimately pose a threat to the male homosocial Arthurian knighthood. This threat is underscored by the emergence of sexual violence, which is touched upon three times in the text. Pushing the boundaries of female roles within one Arthurian text, Wirnt backs off from the possibilities he created within Wigalois in order to reconstruct the patriarchal order. Ultimately, the play on gender roles remains a short-lived experiment and the misogynist overtone in *Wigalois* carries the day. The idea, however, lives on and enables the author of the first Yiddish adaption to create a radically Arthurian utopia.

This chapter both uncovers the positive presentations of female agency that inspire some later adaptors as well as the ways in which Wirnt deconstructs his own experiment at the end. This chapter first explores the two general areas in which women play important roles, mourning and providing clothing, before turning to the discussion of two women who deviate from the model of passivity and attempt to gain additional agency through physical action: the wild woman Ruel and the Amazon Marine, who enable the medieval fascination with female warriors to enter the Arthurian framework. By examining the ways in which women's roles are initially constructed and eventually restricted, we discover an additional paradigm: all women are connected through the trans-religious and -cultural topic of female devotion. In their devotion to a predominantly male counterpart, women are glorified and can even enable intercultural encounters. This chapter's analysis forms the basis for a subsequent analysis of *Wigoleis* and *Viduvilt*, clarifying the later adaptors' narrative choices.

## 2.1 Female Figures between Provision and Devotion

We first consider the classical arenas for female agency that Wirnt honors in his *Wigalois:* supplying the knight with clothing or armor, and excessive mourning. The portrayal of women as providers of clothing and armor is a core motif in medieval vernacular poetry. Women might help dress the hero, equip him with armor or tools, or manufacture these items. Underscoring the power associated with this sartorial responsibility, Wolfram depicts a case in which this power is abused by a female character. Parzival's mother, trying to protect her son from what she fears to be knighthood's deadly fate, exposes her son to ridicule at the Arthurian court by dressing him in fool's clothes (*Parzival* 127, 1–10). Her choice significantly influences his initial reception at the Arthurian court and his eventual path and thus illustrates significant agency. The "father of Arthurian Romance", Chrétien de Troyes, illustrates this motif's darker side in *Yvain* (1180) by portraying 300 women held captive, weaving silk in a workshop without adequate payment (*Yvain* 5298–5324). Courtly ladies' skill has become a commonplace and even turned into a proto-capitalist endeavor for the male captivator. Whereas Wolfram highlights the agency associated with garments, Chrétien reminds his audience of its restrictions, painting a gloomy picture of male exploitation of a core area of women's agency. This traditional courtly woman's skill can be abused and ultimately expropriated by a man.

Wirnt presents a classic, uncritical take on this well-established motif. Women share the responsibility of providing garments and armor with fantastic creatures, such as dwarfs and salamanders, crafting clothes and armor that possess supernatural strength. Multiple scenes depict women presenting the hero with clothes or armor. On the occasion of Wigalois' accolade, for instance, Arthur's queen adheres to tradition and provides Wigalois with the gift of six splendidly crafted and rich outfits (*Wigalois*, 1631). Women don't just provide Wigalois with knightly garments, however, but with clothes in general, as illustrated in a core scene featuring a naked knight. Wounded from his fight with the dragon and robbed of everything by a greedy fisherman and his wife, Wigalois lies completely naked on a lakeshore ("*gewandes alsô lære,*" *Wigalois*, 5799). Lady Beleare, whose husband, Count Moral, Wigalois had saved from a dragon, finds him there. Upon detecting the naked hero, who attempts to cover himself with moss and grass (*Wigalois*, 5919–5920), Lady Beleare takes off her own fur and hands it to Wigalois: "She at once took off and sent to him her coat of flawless calabar, which he quickly put on." ("einen pelz zôch si an der stet ab ir, der was luter grâ; den sande sie dem rîter dâ; hie mit kleite er sich sâ," *Wigalois*, 5937–5940).[3] Later, before leaving the lady's castle to continue his quest, Wigalois requests further garments, particularly armor, from his hostess. Happily, Lady Beleare provides again for the needs of a successful questing knight, including a special harness with a history: a dwarf had forged it for over 30 years before it was stolen from him by an unnamed woman (*Wigalois*, 6079–6081). Eventually, it is Lady Beleare's task to gird Wigalois with his sword, a knight's essential accessory. Upon remarking that some men resent receiving their sword from a woman, the narrator is quick to note that such thoughts are alien to the hero (*Wigalois*, 6196–6203) thus indicating that a woman's essential responsibility of providing garments and armor includes knightly tools. Of course, the "sartorial task" serves the knight on his path but also reflects positively on the knight because his armor and garments are provided by a noble and respectable courtly lady. But it may also be possible to interpret the instances with Lady Beleare

---

[3] English translations are based on *Wigalois. The Knight of Fortune's Wheel* (Thomas 1977).

too positively and overestimate her impact on Wigalois. In the depiction of sartorial responsibility, Wirnt offers a traditional take on the motif, presenting the chore of providing clothing and armor as a noble task for courtly women.

The second and larger area in which women classically establish agency in *Wigalois* is mourning. In this area in *Wigalois*, the limitations and ultimate abandonment of strong female agency in favor of female devotion, passivity, and victimhood become visible. Mourning is a traditional vehicle for women's agency in MHG romances, embodied in the form of excessive grief over the (temporary or final) loss of a husband, lover, or male family member.[4] The better and more noble the lost counterpart, the greater the loss. Thus, this topic as represented in *Wigalois* ultimately becomes a core vehicle in the discourse on male heroism. The mourning in itself is only relevant insofar as it triggers subsequent events. All the adventures in *Wigalois* include or are even initialized by a woman's grief: the messenger maiden sent to the Arthurian court by her queen to request help for a kingdom under siege (*Wigalois*, 1716–1786), a lady lamenting the kidnapping of her price in a beauty contest (*Wigalois*, 2425–2426), the excessively mourning women who accompany the central fight of Wigalois with the red knight (*Wigalois*, 3046–3051), a lady (Beleare) in distress over the loss of her husband (*Wigalois*, 4915–4938) and later over Wigalois' supposed death (*Wigalois*, 5256–5263), a "heathen" wife's (Japhite's) devotion and her death caused by a broken heart, and Lady Liamere's excessive mourning that instigates the epic Namur battle (*Wigalois*, 9983–10037).[5] As lament characterizes all of these ladies' behavior – sometimes in key scenes – and catalyzes the action to follow, Wirnt establishes his female figures within a classical, established motif of courtly romance.

Mourning may lead to redemption if it prompts a knight's action in the traditional damsel-in-distress scenario, but in the context of a woman's devotion to a man, it might also cost her life and thus write her out of the story, as Wirnt reminds its reader implicitly on several occasions. Women's dedication to men is captured by the MHG word *triuwe* (devotion, faithfulness). *Triuwe*, a concept broadly featured in medieval literature, represents a feature innate to all women in *Wigalois*, courtly or not. I understand *triuwe* in this context as selfless devotion and fidelity to a male or female person, related or not, thereby including all women and men within the narrative.[6] Although the predominant form in

---

[4] See, in particular April Lynn Henry's study of female lament in *Tristan*, *Erec*, and the *Nibelungenlied* (Henry 2008, 11–13).
[5] Notice that the mourning crowd after Schaffilun's death includes men (*Wigalois*, 3561–3564).
[6] Hahn (1994, 37) refers to *triuwe* as so-called *minnetriuwe* in *Wigalois*, thereby excluding the devotion of Neraja to her lady, of Florie towards her son Wigalois, or Marine towards her grand-

Wigalois features a woman's devotion to a man, which causes the death of the woman in response to her male counterpart's death, the text also showcases other forms, such as the messenger maiden's fidelity to the queen of the besieged kingdom. Whereas male devotion – often within the framework of fiefdom – requires the men to react proactively and take up arms to protect and avenge the person to whom they are devoted, women in *Wigalois* often cease to exist if the object of their devotion dies or even leaves the realm. Excessive mourning in medieval vernacular literature is performative and not gendered, but dying of grief remains the provenance of women. Wigalois' path is filled with women who die as a consequence of *triuwe*-related mourning, a feature that radically undermines the potential agency that lies in female figures' mourning.

Devotion leading to a woman's death is central to the narrative of Wigalois' mother Florie, the icon for motherly love and devotion: she dies of grief over the loss of her husband Gawein and son Wigalois, a fate common for mothers of MHG heroes.[7] Florie has no say in her son's leaving, but nonetheless tries to convince him to stay and is ridiculed by her son for offering her advice: "A wise man is not governed by a woman's advice." ("Swer sînen rât læt an diu wîp, dern ist ein wîser man." *Wigalois*, 1358–1359). The storyline supports Wigalois' claim that men are wise to ignore women's advice; he leaves for the Arthurian court against his mother's explicit wishes, and subsequently proves to be the perfect knight. As soon as Wigalois' mother has fulfilled her function of producing a male heir and raising him in a courtly manner, she dies. She exists only to ensure the continuation of the line and to raise her son in the absence of the father until Wigalois is old enough to continue his education at another court, where he will meet his father (albeit unknowingly) and become a knight. As a woman without a devotion object, she ceases to matter and is eliminated from the narrative. Her death validates the sincerity of her devotion, a devotion which costs her life and her future significance to the narrative.

*Triuwe*-related mourning presents an inherent conflict in the portrayal of female figures in *Wigalois*. While these women inevitably die, this motif also transcends the ethnocultural and religious background of the figures, as the case of Japhite, wife of the heathen usurper Roaz, illustrates. Japhite is introduced to the audience as a courtly woman, present during the central combat between Wigalois and Roaz. Defeated and mortally wounded by the protagonist, Roaz is taken away by demons, underscoring his evil qualities. Japhite, in contrast, dies of a

---

father. By contrast, Leidinger (2013, 415) points to the significance of the messenger maiden's *triuwe*, which Stange (2012, 138) interprets as agency.

[7] Other famous cases include Tristan's and Parzival's mothers (Stange 2012, 132; Brinker-von der Heyde 1996, 263).

broken heart. Wirnt devotes more than a hundred verses to the praise of Japhite's *triuwe* (*Wigalois*, 7878–8092), which is eventually immortalized in the form of a magnificent memorial. Japhite is buried inside a gigantic red jewel (*Wigalois*, 8230–8231): "[a]round it [this casket] was a large ring of gold into which two clasped hands were wrought to show her loyalty." ("umb diesen sarc wart geleit / von golde ein grôsez vingerlîn: / dar an was ir triuwe schîn–zwô hende nâch der triuwe," *Wigalois*, 7995–8092). An inscription in French and Arabic ("heidnisch," *Wigalois*, 8258) is affixed to Japhite's tomb, communicating her remarkable *triuwe* through a variety of medial channels (*Wigalois*, 8261–8289) and enabling the "heathens" as well as the Christians to commemorate her devotion. Japhite's tomb, as Astrid Lembke highlights, even establishes a temporal place of Christian-"heathen" coexistence: the different groups, Wigalois and his followers as well as the "heathen" cortege, find themselves together in mourning the heathen woman as an ideal representative of *triuwe* (Lembke 2017, 38). The memorial recognizes her devotion and thus underscores how this concept unites ethnocultural groups, so much so that, as Lembke convincingly argues, Japhite's tomb establishes a space for tolerance beyond even Wolfram's *Willehalm* (between 1209 and 1226), which is often hailed as a narrative preaching peaceful coexistence between Christians and "heathens". Japhite's tomb enshrines the connecting strength of female devotion that overcomes even religious-cultural differences.

Although *triuwe* thus represents a strong unifying force, the extensive praise of Japhite's devotion by the narrator and other figures idealizes this form of female behavior, underscoring how the most ideal women in the text – those most praised – will die, generally of a broken heart. Like Wigalois' mother, Japhite soon loses her relevance to the narrative and ceases to exist without the object of her devotion. These women are remembered in *Wigalois* for the devotion that caused their deaths, not for the active role they played in the lives of their sons and husbands. Neither Japhite's nor Florie's mourning leads them to establish active female roles long-term; rather, their *triuwe* and their deaths underscore that their value exists only in relation to a male counterpart.

Wigalois' eventual wife Larie, who shares the character trait of *triuwe* with Florie and Japhite, illustrates that an object of devotion's survival also has no positive impact on women's ability to claim agency. Whereas Japhite dies just after her husband succumbs to his mortal combat wounds, Wigalois survives the duel and thus remains Larie's focus of devotion, ensuring her continued existence in the narrative. After defeating Roaz, the central task of Wigalois' quest, the knight is reunited with Larie. In a display of strong devotion, she accompanies Wigalois to his final battle against Count Lion of Namur in a tower-like structure on the back of an elephant, safeguarded by well-known and distinguished Arthurian knights Iwein and Erec (*Wigalois*, 10645). Larie's tower becomes the final and conclusive icon for women's passivity in *Wigalois*, despite the brief moments of agency.

In her article on the Namur campaign, Cora Dietl suggests that this final epic battle is staged as a chess game, with the battlefield as a chessboard (Dietl 2002, 105). An elephant carrying a tower is a pre-modern, oriental element of chess dating back to Chaturanga, an Indian chess-predecessor that included a piece featuring an elephant carrying a battle fortification. In the Middle Ages, the elephant faded away, leaving behind only the tower, or what we nowadays know as the rook or castle. In her tower on the elephant's back, Larie becomes a chess piece on the board of a battle orchestrated by Wigalois. Immobilized inside the portable tower, Larie remains alive but is a completely passive presence while male knights actively fight. Rather than being made a queen and thus becoming a relevant piece on the board, she is enclosed within a different piece and protected by two other pieces, knights. Traditionally, a chess player would have two knights available. The two knights in this case, Erec and Iwein, whom a contemporary audience would recognize as core figures in the Arthurian world and therefore intertextual references, are placed next to Larie's tower, underscoring *Wigalois*' gender divide, which immobilizes women and removes them from the text should they lose their object of devotion. The agency of female mourning and the trans-cultural utopia enabled by *triuwe* remain a brief experiment within the text, abandoned in favor of female passivity and immobility.

## 2.2 "Against Her Will": Sexual Violence Against Women in *Wigalois*

After *triuwe*, sexual violence is the second reoccurring motif in *Wigalois* that impacts gender relations and is associated predominantly with women. The first two instances of sexual violence in *Wigalois* illustrate that the topic is only introduced to discuss a knight's flawlessness, in one case Gawein's and in the other Wigalois'. The third instance, discussed in the next section, serves as a reminder of what happens if women actively seize agency: they become grotesque figures, portrayed as overstepping boundaries and disregarding elementary knightly codes of honor.

The topic of sexual violence in the context of a medieval Arthurian romance is by no means unique to *Wigalois*. It often appears as a theme, though not a main topic, in Arthurian romances, becoming a vehicle through which social issues are discussed and critiques of certain societal practices and norms are displayed (Classen 2011, 231). Despite condemning the use of sexual violence, courtly fiction instrumentalizes the topic within knightly logic. As Gravdal points out: "Chrétien's romances teach that rape is wrong [...]. But they simultaneously aestheticize rape as a formulaic challenge: potential assaults are set up at regular narrative intervals so that knights can prove their mettle. The audience is led to ignore the literal consequences of violence against women." (Gravdal 1991, 44).[8] Chrétien and Hartmann von Aue include (impending) sexual violence in *Erec* repeatedly, often under the veil of efforts by counts to marry the heroine Enite.[9] By contrast, *Wigalois* includes a scene of sexual violence within a comical framework, to critique the lack of societal order, in this case involving a woman who attempts to seize power. Although scholars have discussed *Wigalois*' three scenes of sexual violence, they have rarely approached them in connection to women's agency or lack thereof. Analyzing these scenes within a framework of gender and power is key to understanding how the text utilizes women as victims in order to discuss knightly perfection or warn against transgressive women seizing agency.

The first instance of sexual violence appears only in a brief and seemingly subsidiary remark within the Stone of Virtue scene, a virtue test for Wigalois. As the narrator of *Wigalois* explains, the Stone of Virtue has a supernatural quality; only a person who has never done anything immoral is able to sit on it. The motif appears in several MHG texts, including Ulrich von Zatzikhoven's *Lanzelet* (after 1194/1200), and serves as the ultimate "character" test for a noble knight.[10] Several German and Yiddish adaptations of *Wigalois* retain this motif and use it to discuss the relationship between father and son.

The *Wigalois* narrator lists only two people able to sit on the Stone of Virtue: King Arthur and Wigalois. But the audience soon learns that a third figure is able at least to touch the stone: "Sir Gawein could stretch his hand out to it, but that was all. I'll tell you why: as I have often heard, he once laid hands on a pretty maiden against her will, so that she cried out and wept." ("her Gâwein der

---

[8] Gravdal further explains: "Courtly romance discovers in the representation of rape a space where the audience can enjoy the taboo pleasure of a titillating scene without transgressing romance decorum. The moral and social complexities raised by erotic moments work to deflect attention away from the pleasure of imagining violence against the female body. [...] Far from empowering a female audience, Arthurian romance transforms rape into a romantic adventure: the heroine who is subjected to the threat of assault both enjoys the great compliment of her beauty and basks in the reflected glory of the triumphant knight who protects her." (1991, 67).
[9] Because Enite is repeatedly victimized, including by her husband, scholarship has debated at length whether Hartmann uses her to criticize the courtly society's treatment of women. For examples see Klein 2002, 433–463; Wandhoff 1996, 170–189; and Classen 1993, 25–42.
[10] Such tests of virtue, used to make unseen qualities and abilities visible, can be traced back to Celtic, antique, and oriental influences (Kasper 1995, 13, 41).

reichte dar / mit der hant, und niht baz; / Ich sagiu wie er verworhte daz / er zem steine niht moht komen, / als ichz hân vernomen: / eine maget wol getân / die greif er über ir willen an, / sô daz sie weinde unde schrê [sic!]," *Wigalois*, 1506–1513). Due to having touched a girl against her will, Gawein cannot sit on the stone. The scene is not further explained, and the audience is left to interpret what "touching against her will" actually implies, especially given that the girl expresses her disapproval with screams and tears.[11]

It is notable that although the incident with the maiden keeps the otherwise model knight from sitting on the stone, the narrator is anxious to restore Gawein's reputation: "He never did anything else improper from his childhood to his death; however, this kept him from the stone." ("deheiner slahte untugent mê / er von sîner kindheit nie / unz an sînen tôt begie; / die selbe in zuo dem steine niht lie," *Wigalois*, 1514–1517). Within *Wigalois* this is the only scene in which Gawein's conduct and character are questioned.

Wirnt's choice in this scene is not dictated by the genre of Arthurian romance. In other texts, such as Ulrich von Zatzikhoven's *Lanzelet*, Gawein remains perfectly virtuous, able to sit on the Stone of Virtue (*Lanzelet*, 5177–5178) which aligns with a portrayal of Gawein as a perfect knight in the MHG and Old French Arthurian traditions. Chrétien's Gawein (Old French: Gauvain) even supplies the wisdom and the strength the king frequently lacks, and Hartmann von Aue continues this tradition (Kasper 1995, 256; Thomas 1987, 55–56). By contrast, in contemporaneous French post-Chrétien romances, Gawain's reputation deteriorates in accordance with the whole courtly atmosphere, especially in the French prose texts such as the *Queste del Saint Graal* [Quest for the Holy Grail] (a section of the Prose Lancelot / Vulgate Cycle, thirteenth century). These texts "associate Gauvain with overtly evil activities [...], the duality already inherent in the natural affinity to casual liaisons with women attributed to him from early on in the tradition" (Quinlan 2013, 53). Wolfram's Gawein (in *Parzival*) comes the closest to Wirnt's depiction, as he is known for amorous adventures that can cause a woman grief.

The *Wigalois* narrator only problematizes the behavior temporarily but still places his knight in the tradition of the "perfect Gawein"-narratives of his predecessors rather than on the negative ones of his contemporaries. Gawein is, after all, able to touch the stone even if he cannot sit on it. Besides the episode with the young maiden, the *Wigalois* narrator attests that Gawein never expressed any "negative virtue" ("untugend", *Wigalois*, 1514). Gawein thus remains at least an

---

11 Classen, Eming, and Jaeger interpret Gawein's behavior as rape (Classen 2007, 452; Jaeger 2000, 237; Eming 1999, 163).

almost perfect hero. Stephan Fuchs and Jutta Eming explain this scene by examining the dilemma Wirnt faced when establishing Wigalois' character as the son of a perfect knight (Eming 1999, 165; Fuchs 1997, 122).[12] By adding this "minimal" blemish while simultaneously emphasizing Gawein's otherwise flawless character, the narrator's aim is merely to turn Gawein into the second-best, almost-perfect knight and therewith mark the main hero of the text, Wigalois, as the best of all knights – in line with King Arthur himself.

The scholarly debate about this scene mirrors an important fact within the narrative itself. The focus of the debate lies on the question of Gawein's character, not on the victim. In this sense, the emphasis on Gawein underscores the core feature of the representation of sexual violence within *Wigalois:* the female victims do not matter but are rather secondary figures that enable a necessary solution to the text's problem of featuring two perfect knights in the same narrative. If, however, we focus on the lack of female agency in this scene and its relevance to the narrative, we realize that the girl has no agency, and her reputation is insignificant. In the fight between giant and knight, women become mere objects of the male gaze and are relegated to the background of the conflict (Boyer 2016, 49). Sarah Westphal-Wihl argues similarly that rape in classical Arthurian literature can turn the audience away from the consequences of sexual violence and "focus its attention on the chivalric dilemmas of male feudal culture" (Westphal-Wihl, 92–93). *Wigalois* includes scenes of violence against women not to demonstrate that justice for these women (and their humanity) should be a concern. Instead, these scenes simply emphasize the relative virtue of its (more important) male knight characters.[13] Women are, therefore, instrumentalized to the development of men.

The second incident of sexual violence in *Wigalois* does not lead the narrator to an explicit condemnation of such an act either, but rather turns the situation into a reflection on accomplished knighthood. Different scene, same topic: the reinforcement of the knight's virtue. Riding through the woods on their way to the bewitched kingdom of Korntin, Wigalois, the messenger maiden Neraja, and Neraja's servant dwarf perceive "[a] voice, miserable and wrathful" ("stimme / klägelîch und grimme," *Wigalois*, 2041–2042). The voice, as it turns out, belongs to a maiden in the forest who has been abducted by two giants who are about to rape her:

---

**12** Thomas argues that Wirnt tries to rehabilitate Gawein in light of *Parzival* and other texts (Thomas 2005, 84), and that Wigalois finally rehabilitates Gawein by inviting his father to his wedding festivities (Thomas 2004, 108).
**13** Kasper points out that downplaying Gawein's guilt implies an immense disregard for women and violence against women (Kasper 1995, 257).

> Two mighty giants [were] sitting by a fire in a clearing at the shore of a lake [...]. Sad to say, they were fondling a maiden, against her will and could not silence her with either plea or threat. The caressing was very hard on her, for she was much too weak for them. But they intended to do their will with her whether she liked it or not. [...] One [of the giants] was pressing her to him with both arms.
>
> ("sitzen zwêne starke risen / bî einem viure ûf den wisen [...] / einer juncvrouwen si dâ pflâgen / leider über ir willen. / sine mohten si niht gestillen / mit deheiner slahte bet: / daz trûten ir unsanfte tet, / wan sie was in gar ze kranc. / sus wolden si über ir danc / ir willen mit ir gehabet hân; [...]/ si hêt mit beiden armen / der eine an sich gedrücket."
> Wigalois, 2065–2066, 2068–2075, 2078–2079)

The maiden's only agency in that moment remains in her lament, which attracts the attention of Wigalois. The Arthurian knight realizes the necessity for immediate help, in stark contrast to the messenger maiden Neraja who is reluctant to take any further action. By the end of this incident, our protagonist has completed his first true knightly task.[14] The maiden's vocalized mourning functions as a trigger for the knight, whose task reinforces a classic motif: saving a damsel in distress. The damsel in distress herself, in accordance with the previously discussed scene, is insignificant, and interchangeable with other such women.

Within the moral logic of the text, this situation is made less controversial for the audience than the Gawein incident, as it is marked by an additional transgression: un-courtly creatures assaulting a courtly lady. But instead of condemning the violence itself, the scene becomes a vehicle for the narrator to praise women while, at the same time, objectifying them as it includes two longer reflections: one on women being the cause of men's true happiness (*Wigalois*, 2091–2108), and one on a glorified past, when breaking an oath was still a despicable crime, in contrast with the present (*Wigalois*, 2146–2158).[15] The giants' attempted rape itself is downplayed.

The incident becomes the first and thus central situation that showcases Wigalois' knightly skills. It serves as an aptitude test, which he passes with flying colors, before the main adventure: bringing salvation to bewitched Korntin. The fact that Wigalois comprehends the danger and reacts without hesitation to the classic damsel-in-distress scenario marks him immediately as the perfect knight, at least in the eyes of an audience familiar with courtly romances. Not so for Neraja, the messenger maiden. From the moment in which she "acquired" only Wi-

---

**14** It seems strange that only Wigalois, but not the messenger maiden Neraja, cares about violence against the virgin. Classen argues that Neraja's mind is set on that greater violence in Korntin (Classen 2007, 438).
**15** Similarly, Busch and Thomas argue that the discourse in *Wigalois* is tied to lamenting an idealized and long gone past (Busch 2011, 137–138; Thomas 2005, 82).

galois' support for saving her bewitched home country under usurpation by the heathen Roaz, she was displeased. Instead of returning home with an experienced and (also intertextually) well-known Arthurian knight, she gets Wigalois: a mere boy who was raised by his mother in an unspecified otherworld and who has no knightly experience whatsoever, who only recently reached the Arthurian court to find his father. Neraja perceives Wigalois as too inexperienced and too young – a knight without a beard, even!

Focused only on the task of acquiring a savior for her country, Neraja is reluctant to aid the woman in distress when she hears her screams. This reluctance works in favor of the audience's positive perception of Wigalois in two ways: Neraja, who has dismissed Wigalois, is portrayed as unempathetic to a stranger's distress, and she is proven wrong in her judgment of him as a deficient knight. The attempted rape of the maiden underscores Wigalois' knightly skills as he fights with the giants and foreshadows his success in the central fight with the heathen giant Roaz. Featuring sexual violence as narratological strategy emphasizes the lesson of this scene: that Wigalois is the perfect knight, eminently suitable for the tasks that await him.

## 2.3 Wild Women: *Wigalois*' Transgressive Women

The third episode featuring sexual violence subverts the established motif, presenting us not with a female victim but instead with an Arthurian knight in distress. On his way to fight his main opponent, the heathen Roaz, Wigalois encounters Ruel, a woman living alone in the forest. Scholars have often discussed Ruel in the context of religion, perceiving her as a demonic figure in an alliance with all the other "dark" or "evil" creatures in the text (Häberlein 2012, 81–82; Henderson 1986, 103). But the Ruel episode provides a crucial means of teaching the audience how to differentiate between appropriate and transgressional women's behavior in *Wigalois*, an outcome the narrator achieves by turning the inverted motif into comic relief.

Already the fact that she lives in the forest marks Ruel as an uncourtly lady. Her physical features are described as monstrous:

> Her hair was long and tangled and hung down to her hips. Her head was large, her nose flat, and her eyes gleamed forth like two candles from the mass of hair. Her brows were bushy and gray. She had large teeth, a broad mouth and two doglike ears which hung down for nearly a foot. [...] Her breasts hung down against her sides like two large satchels.

> ("ir hâr enpflohten unde lanc, / zetal in ir buoc ez swanc. / daz houbet grôz, ir nase vlach. / daz wîp ûz grôzer riuhe sach / als zwô kerzen brünnen dâ. / ir brâ lanc unde grâ, / grôze

zene, wîten munt; / zwei ôren hêt si al sein hunt, / diu hingen nider spanne breit. / [...] ir brüste nider hiengen: / die sîten si beviengen / gelîch zwein grôzen taschen dâ." / *Wigalois*, 6292–6300, 6314–6316)

Rather than comparing Ruel to the Holy Grail's messenger maiden Cundrie in *Parzival*, which would seem to be the obvious choice considering Ruel's grotesque physical features, the *Wigalois*' narrator draws from Arthurian depictions of courtly and beautiful ladies such as Enite, from Hartmann von Aue's *Erec*, and Jeschute, from Wolfram's *Parzival:* "Whoever had his pride and joy from her never saw Lady Enite. [...] [H]er body was not like that of Lady Jeschute." ("hêt iemen von ir hôhen muot, dern sach der vrouwen Ênîten niht, [...] ir lîp der vrouwen Jeschûten [...] was ungelîch." *Wigalois*, 6307–6308, 6325–6326). These women already contrast with women in *Wigalois* since they possess significant agency. Enite, for example, repeatedly warns Erec against impending danger and thus saves not just the Arthurian knight but also herself. Notably, the narrator refers to Jeschute but not the grail messenger Cundrie whose physical features, such as her bear-like ears, dog-like nose and the substantial facial hear (*Parzival* 313, 17–314, 11), stand in stark contrast to her wisdom and status within the grail society. Her physical features mislead Parzival and the audience at a first glance, playing with their expectations in regard to *Kalos kagathos*, the platonic idea that a character's outer beauty reflects her inner beauty. Wirnt presents a classic take on this concept: a lady cannot be as ugly as Ruel (and live in the uncourtly sphere of the forest) and at the same time be essentially courtly and good. Tying the concept of beauty to courtly love (MHG: *minne*), the narrator states that a night spent with Ruel makes men age rapidly: "A short night would make an old man out of him who lay with her, so sweet was her love." ("ein kurziu naht diu machet in alt / swer bî ir solde sîn gelegen; / so süezer minne kunde si pflegen," *Wigalois*, 6350–6352). The contrast between Ruel's monstrous features and the ideal beauty of the courtly lady, as well as of sweet courtly love ("süezer minne"), constitutes the basis for Ruel's function as comic relief.[16]

Miscommunication, or a clash of codes, provokes other examples of humor in the encounter between Wigalois and Ruel, which results in the passivity of the Arthurian knight. Wigalois adheres to the knightly code of honor, refusing to draw a sword against a woman: "because his heart was always moved with great valor and he did not think he would ever need to use his sword against

---

[16] Although in general it is difficult to uncover humor in texts from the past, there are certain criteria, as Klaus Schwind explains, such as the unusual combination of separate elements by describing the uncourtly Ruel through a comparison with courtly ladies (Schwind 2001, 333). Regarding medieval laughter, see Velten 2005, 125–144.

her." ("si endûhte in des niht wert / daz er gegen ir sîn swert / immer gevuorte, / wan grôziu tugent ruorte /sîn herze zallen stunden." *Wigalois*, 6373–6377). However, as Ruel does not adhere to a knightly code, she initiates a fight and subsequently renders the heroic knight powerless by means of her own strength. This in itself marks a radical transgression and enables the audience to deem her actions inappropriate and transgressive.

This scene is not simply portrayed as a fight between two opponents, an uncourtly woman and a knight, but it is rife with sexual metaphors. Ruel takes possession of Wigalois' sword: "She tore his sword from his side." ("si zôch im ûz sîn eigen swert," *Wigalois*, 6417), indicating an emasculation of the hero-as-knight in two ways. First, the sword is a phallic object in a scene filled with sexual dialogue. Böcking analyzes this imagery further, arguing that the woman's possession of the sword in combination with the man lying on the floor inverts conventional sexual roles (Böcking 2013, 373). Secondly, Ruel deprives Wigalois of an object that is essential to his identity as a (male) knight. Whereas Böcking emphasizes the seriousness of the scene in the context of breaking a taboo (Böcking 2013, 371), I argue that the narrator's initial description of Ruel, in which he evokes courtly ladies and sweet courtly love, establishes a comical framework for this encounter. The narrator also describes Wigalois' defeat in a comic way: Ruel fetters Wigalois and drags him away like a sack ("This ugly woman bore him off like a sack." ["diu selbe vrouwe ungemeit truoc in hin als einen sac"], *Wigalois*, 6384–6385). The hero is carried away not just unheroically by a woman but also in a fashion that marks the woman as behaving not accordingly to her gender ("un-maidenly"). Thus, comic relief originates from the subversion of expected gender roles, the comparison of the defeated knight with a sack, and the figure of a fighting woman, who is particularly strong and drags away her victim.

Ruel takes an active position within this scene, and the subsequent fight is described in terms reminiscent of forced intercourse, but with the woman dominating the male hero. By alluding to the rape of a man, the narrator references a medieval motif that is usually perceived within a comical framework (often through jokes about sexual positions or male pregnancy), such as in the MHG humoresque short stories called *Mæren*.[17] A classic representative of the genre, the short story "Des Mönches Not" [The Monk's Suffering] (early thirteenth century), tells the "cautionary tale" of a young monk who attains his entire educa-

---

[17] Heinrich Wittenwiler's *Ring* (1408/10) represents a special case. Here, the repeated rape of Mätzli and other women is used to illustrate a topsy-turvy world, accompanied by general misogynist stereotypes, such as the idea that women have unsatisfiable sexual appetites (Classen 2011, 154).

tion – including sex education—through reading books. Eager to experience what he has learned in reality; the young man is taught about sex by a woman (presumably a prostitute) who rapes him. Due to confusion about inverted sexual positions (a classic trope already established in antiquity), the monk believes that he is pregnant as the result of what can only be perceived as rape. The resulting fear of pregnancy is ingrained in the fear of a man being dominated by a woman and impregnated by her. Thus, these two fears fuel each other: while conception and domination are linked in this belief system, the sexually dominated individual could get pregnant. Despite the fact that no explicit medieval discourse on raping men existed, both stories draw on the inversion of the accepted order within sexual practices in order to achieve comic relief. In *Wigalois,* the inclusion of this trope helps us understand the construction of women's agency or lack thereof. After having established the motif of sexual violence more traditionally within the giant-maiden scene, Wirnt upends the motif, using the attempted rape of a man to evoke humor among a medieval audience.[18] The sexual transgression and attempted rape cause comic relief but also serve as a cautionary tale essential to understanding Wirnt's ultimate return to idealizing the passive, devoted female figure: women seizing agency subvert the socially accepted order.

Despite Ruel's contrasting portrayal, even she is connected to all other women in *Wigalois,* including courtly, well-appraised ladies like Beleare, Japhite, Liamere, and Florie, through the motif of *triuwe.* Ruel's actions towards Wigalois are motivated by revenge for the murder of her husband: "Her husband's name was Feroz. He had been slain by Flojir of Belamunt. [...] This was how she lost her dear mate and she wanted revenge." ("Ferôz geheizen was ir man. / den sluoc Flojîr von Belamunt. / [...] sus verlôs si ir lieben man; / des wolde si in engelten lân," *Wigalois,* 6356–6357, 6361–6362). Yet, in contrast to the other women who trust courtly knights to aid and avenge them, Ruel acts on her own behalf, and therefore eventually fails. Exploring the non-normative role of Ruel, Böcking argues that Larie becomes the model for all other female figures in the text. In contrast, Ruel presents the worst female character by deviating the most from Larie (Böcking 2013, 380). The text punishes active women as their agency ultimately renders men powerless and puts them in a stereotypical feminine position, which comes at the cost of socially accepted practiced and the established order. Jutta Eming interprets Ruel's ugliness as connected to her activeness

---

**18** In contemporary discourses on rape, particularly in legal cases, the term "sexual assault" is often preferred as a "reconfiguration that serves to place rape on a continuum of sexual violence but ultimately refuses its specificity." (Cahill 2001, 11).

(Eming 1999, 200). Although the wild woman is not explicitly marked as a giant, she represents several observations made by Tina Marie Boyer about the giant in medieval literature. Boyer points out that, albeit rare creatures, female giants are depicted as more bestial and ferocious than their male counterparts (Boyer 2016, 6, 28). Unlike Japhite and Florie, the agency-seizing Ruel is not portrayed as an ideal, beautiful lady to be remembered for her *triuwe*, but rather as a transgressive woman who upends the world. Therefore, these women, as narrated in the case of Ruel, present a threat to the male homosocial society of Arthurian knighthood in *Wigalois*. Similar to Boyer's argument that the giant's representation of *superbia* threatening courtly order needs to be defeated, Ruel needs to be defeated in order to preserve the courtly world's existence in harmony (Boyer 2016, 223). By turning Ruel into a figure of comic relief, the narrator ensures that the audience can simply laugh at her attempts to seize agency despite her being, in many ways, an intriguing and powerful female figure. Her appeal is such that she serves as Wigalois' main adversary in the *Viduvilt* adaptation.

The second fighting woman in *Wigalois*, the Amazon Marine, underscores Ruel's portrayal as transgressive and not adhering to courtly standards. Ruel and Marine are both portrayed as independent women who take a man's place in the context of combat: Ruel, in a direct fight with Wigalois; Marine as part of an army. The central difference lies in their sexuality: where Ruel is portrayed as overly sexually active, Marine leads a celibate group of 12 women, all initially heathens but eventually converted to Christianity (*Wigalois*, 9135). Repeatedly, the text emphasizes Marine's virginity, which remains intact until her death.[19] Marine's virginity embodies the concepts of *triuwe* and mourning.[20] Grieving the loss of her grandfather, Adan, who was abducted by Roaz (*Wigalois*, 9150–9164), she seizes agency by choosing to be a virgin fighter – a decision with fatal consequences.

The audience meets Marine in the context of the epic Namur battle, the same battle that Larie attends in her elephant-tower. In contrast to Larie, a strictly passive observer protected by two famous knights, Marine actively fights. They represent simultaneously the fear and dream of female autonomy (Clover 1986, 49). The Amazon's knightly aspirations are marked as unwomanly, both explicitly and implicitly. After her introduction (*Wigalois*, 9165–9177), she is contrasted with queen Elamie: "Queen Elamie rode as women do." ("vrouwe Êlamîe, diu künigîn, vuor nâch wîplîchem sit," *Wigalois*, 9178–9179) Marine, on the other

---

[19] Due to Marine's age and virginity, Carol J. Clover suggests the name "maiden warrior" rather than "Amazon" in the context of similar narratives (Clover 1986, 36).
[20] As Maria E. Müller argues, Marine shares the combination of virility and virginity with similar women in antiquity and medieval literature (Müller 1995, 17).

hand, takes any opportunity to fight like a knight and even defeats real knights in jousting (*Wigalois*, 9166–9171). By marking her behavior as unmaidenly, the text reiterates the idea of battle as a quintessentially masculine affair (McLaughlin 1990, 195). Therefore, the *Wigalois* narrator explicitly and implicitly ensures that the audience interprets Marine's choice to actively participate in combat as inappropriate for a woman. Wirnt plays a double game, participating in the subversive fascination with Amazons and female warriors while adhering to a strict moral framework of appropriate women's behavior by marking Marine's choices as ultimately unwomanly.

One way to address Marine's transgressive behavior would be to present her in a humorous way. The audience has, after all, already encountered Ruel as an active woman and seen the negative consequences of such behavior through her comedic, derisive interpretation. However, the narrator deals with the Amazon in a different way. Marine represents male authors' fascination with the female fighter tribe – beginning with the first Amazon queen, Otrera, and her daughter, Penthesilea, who fought in the Trojan War. Due to the broad appeal of such figures from antiquity, Amazons are prominently featured in the *matière de Rome*, stories pertaining to antiquity, such as Heinrich von Veldeke's *Eneas* (around 1170) and romances about Alexander the Great. According to the Old French poet Jean Bodel (1165–1210) the three dominant narratological traditions in medieval literature are *matière de Rome* (stories pertaining to antiquity), *matière de Bretagne* (stories pertaining to king Arthur and his knights), and *matière de France* (stories pertaining to Charlemagne's fight against the heathens). Other figures from *matière de Rome* narratives already appear in the Otherworld of Korntin, such as Marrien, a centaur-like creature ("beidiu man unde ros," *Wigalois*, 7023) posed to protect Roaz's castle. Wigalois slays Marrien on the way to the show-down with Roaz. The centaur and the Amazon, as representatives of the *matière de Rome,* illustrate Wirnt's integration of elements from other motif repositories. The case of the female warrior shows Wirnt going to great lengths to include a wide array of female figures but ultimately subordinating even the female warrior to overarching concerns for "appropriate areas" of female activity.

But the virgin Amazons, who chose their status themselves, pose a problem for medieval texts; in contrast with idealized courtly ladies, they cannot be integrated into the patriarchal world of such narratives in general nor into Wirnt's world of female passivity and *triuwe* in particular. The texts attempt to integrate these figures in two possible ways, as Maria E. Müller proposes: in almost all cases, the Amazon woman either loses her virginity or loses her identity through death (Müller 1995, 22). The most prominent Amazon representative from MHG literature, Queen Camilla from Veldeke's *Eneas*, has to die in order for the text to reconstitute the appropriate sexual-social order (Müller 1995, 242). Marine suffers a similar fate in the battle of Namur: "The maiden thus displayed every virtue until a sharp spear cut her away. It was thrust by in a joust with Duke Galopear of Greece, who aimed at her breast and threw her down dead." ("sus lebd diu maget schône mit vil ganzer werdicheit, unz si ein scharfez sper vernseit. daz treip ein helt mit joste dar, der herzoge Galopêar; von Kriechen was er geborn; ûf die brust hêt ers erkorn und valte die maget tôte nider." *Wigalois*, 11023–11030). With Marine's death on the battlefield, the second fighting woman with significant agency is removed from the narrative. Moreover, Marine is not remembered for her qualities on the battlefield, but for her *triuwe* to her grandfather – who, after the battle is won, returns her corpse to her homeland, Alarie (*Wigalois*, 12273–11275). Here, the attention shifts to remembering Marine for her devotion and faithfulness to a man rather than for her knightly deeds. This final example of an active woman in the text reinforces the impression that Wirnt's *Wigalois* offers no integration of women who exceed their supposedly accepted roles within the Arthurian-Christian courtly world despite clearly benefiting from the fascinating possibilities they offer for the conception of his romance. They are ridiculed or they die.

## 2.4 Conclusion

Marine's death concludes Wirnt's experiment with a broad variety of female figures that couldn't be more different but are overall united in the topic of *triuwe*, portrayed as a powerful force that transcends ethnocultural and religious boundaries. *Triuwe* is both a blessing and a curse for these female figures, as it underscores female devotion but also shows that their *raison d'être* is men. *Triuwe*, the female devotion to a (mostly) male object, is central to the depiction of women in *Wigalois* and results in the death of a female character in response to her male counterpart's loss. Whereas masculine *triuwe*, often within the framework of fiefdom, requires men to react proactively and take up arms in order to protect and avenge the object of their devotion, women in *Wigalois* often cease to exist if the object of their devotion dies or even just leaves their realm. Thus, dedication to men significantly restricts the agency of the diverse female figures in *Wigalois*.

Several of Wirnt's women are portrayed as powerful figures who, nonetheless, succumb to the overarching passivity of the ideal woman within the logic of *Wigalois*. Moreover, the text deploys violence against women in order to showcase the knight's abilities. The depiction of women in *Wigalois* as passive others, objects on the knight's path to a successful quest, is by no means representative of contemporaneous Arthurian literature, but rather presents an extreme: a choice that results from Wirnt's focus on Wigalois' perfection in his quest.

Women in Hartmann von Aue's *Erec* and *Iwein*, Wolfram's *Parzival*, and Gottfried von Straßburg's *Tristan*[21], all written around 1200, have significantly more agency that exceeds the areas of mourning and providing clothing and armor, without being ridiculed or removed from these romances. Although lacking ultimate agency, women in Wirnt's *Wigalois* represent a broader diversity than many of his contemporaries. But eventually, Wirnt retreats from using these women to challenge the conception of Arthurian patriarchal society and returns instead to classical tropes and representations of the ultimate ideal: courtly femininity.

The following two chapters show how two adaptors took Wirnt's portrayal of female figures in entirely different directions, one fortifying the ideal of female passivity and the other creating the utopian society for which Wirnt did not push. The preceding analysis of the conflicted *Wigalois* narrative enables us to understand how two adaptations, which could not represent women more differently, originated in one shared text, each representing significant choices of the adaptors that underscore their respective works' identities as unique entities, acts of (re)creation, and acts of reception.

---

**21** Alexandra Sterling-Hellenbrand argues that in Hartmann von Aue's *Erec* and *Iwein*, Wolfram von Eschenbach's *Parzival* and Gottfried von Straßburg's *Tristan*, women's agency is not granted but is negotiable (Sterling-Hellenbrand 2001, xv). In the case of *Tristan*, as Ann Marie Rasmussen has shown, women's agency stands in direct conflict with the dominant medieval clerical conventions.

# 3 *Wigoleis:* Mother Mary's Maidens

> May God grant the work's successful conclusion. I set my hope in His divine grace and His kind mother that they will help me bring this work to a good end, as nobody is capable of achieving anything without their help.[1]
>
> ("Got wőll das die [arbeit] såligklichen volpracht werde/ als ich in hoffnung seinen gőtlichen genaden/ vnd seiner lieben můter getrawe sie helffen mir dises werck zů eim gůtem ende bringen dann ye niemant on ir hilff nichtzen volbringen mag." *Wigoleis*, Aiiv)[2]

In the opening to *Wigoleis vom Rade* (1493/1519), a prose adaptation of Wirnt's *Wigalois*, the narrator entrusts his work into divine hands, a classic trope common in medieval and early modern vernacular literature that displays humility as well as a familiarity with literary conventions.[3] Divine powers are evoked in this opening, specifically including God as well as "his kind mother." The inclusion of God's mother in this classical trope represents a major selling point for a contemporaneous audience and is a core feature of *Wigoleis*. Mother Mary is this text's central female role model, informing especially its portrayal of the hero's mother (here: Florye), and offering guidance to the narrator and the titular hero himself. The idealization of Mary as role model continues throughout the narrative but does not lead to the inclusion of strong female figures. Rather, with Mary, *Wigoleis* reinforces the tale of female normative submissive roles because she serves predominantly to underscore the hero's messianic character and thus helps to shift the focus even more towards the male hero of the text. As a consequence, female figures retreat entirely to the background, becoming an audience that admires Arthurian chivalry and knightly aptitude. We will see that the implicit conventionalization of feminine norms taking place in *Wigalois* is amplified in the early modern text but materializes in a different form. The adaptor narrows the ideal of female devotion to mere admiration, which manifests most strongly in the pictorial program of the adaptation.

Written more than 200 years after Wirnt's *Wigalois*, *Wigoleis* was completed in 1483 but published for the first time ten years later by the famous printer Jo-

---

[1] For his help with translating the intricacies of the Early New High German spirit into modern English, I thank my wonderful colleague Ellwood Wiggins.
[2] The first pages of the 1483/1493 print are missing and therewith the title. The second, most popular edition will form the center of my analysis.
[3] Note the changed name here: from Wigalois to Wigoleis. The spelling of the name alternates throughout the text between Wigoleys and Wigoleis.

https://doi.org/10.1515/9783110624403-004

hann Schönsperger (1455–1521) in Augsburg.⁴ The second edition (1519), printed by Johann Knoblauch in Strasbourg, became the more popular version and is the only complete, preserved version of this adaptation, titled *Ein gar schŏne liepliche und kurtzweilige History Von dem Edelen herren Wigoleis vom Rade. Ein Ritter von der Tafelronde. Mit seinen schŏnen hystorien und figuren/ Wie er geborn/ vnnd sein leben von seiner jugent an Biß an sein ende gefürt vnnd vollbracht hat* [A very nice and entertaining tale about the noble Sir Wigoleis of the Wheel, a knight of the Round Table. With pretty stories and images. How he was born, and how he led and completed his life from his youth until its end.].⁵ Knoblauch both printed and reworked the first part of Schönsperger's *Wigoleis* thoroughly. Knoblauch's 1519 edition, being widely known, is the basis of my analysis in this chapter.

Scholars have not yet discovered the actual author of the *Wigoleis* prose adaptation. Likewise, because of the text's supra-regional language, the place of composition remains unknown (Flood 2000, 773). It has been argued that the text itself became the template for another adaptation, the retelling within *Buch der Liebe* [Book of Love] (1587), Sigmund Feyerabend's anthology of early modern prose novels (Weidenmüller 1910, 2; Flood 2000, 769). Wigalois narratives were incredibly popular in the fifteenth and sixteenth centuries; a third adaptation of the story was included in the Arthurian anthology Ulrich Füetrer's *Buch der Abenteuer der Ritter von der Tafelrunde* [Book about the Adventures of the Knights of the Roundtable] (1496–1500). Though *Wigoleis* appears as prose, in accordance with the fashion of early modern adaptations of MHG material, Füetrer returned the narrative to its original, medieval verse form.

Previously, scholars perceived *Wigoleis* as deficient in comparison to Wirnt's *Wigalois*, idealizing the vernacular literature of the High Middle Ages in contrast to the so-called early modern prose literature ("Volksbücher").⁶ This approach to

---

4 In the fifteenth century, the Augsburg workshop was one of the leading publishing houses (Ader 2010, 20).
5 Schönhoff offers a good overview of the missing sections (Schönhoff 2008, 371–374). One reason for the ten years that passed between the writing and the first print edition was that Knoblauch strongly reworked the style of the first version. Yet, he added such descriptive writing only for the first section, not the complete text. Flood speculates that perhaps Knoblauch wanted to rework the model, but ran out of time, or lost interest (Flood 2000, 775–776).
6 For decades, non-religious novels written between the fifteenth and seventeenth centuries have been referred to with the term "Volksbücher" ("people's books"). Yet this term has been criticized for its romantic implications and focus on the audience. The term also tends to include fiction novels as well as recipes, presenting a rather heterogeneous assembly of texts. In recent decades the term "early modern prose novels" has been established to refer to the non-religious, fiction novels from this time, composed in prose and often-subtitled "histori." Jan-Dirk Müller makes a case for the term "prose novel" as a category that is both precise and flexible and

early modern prose novels has been slowly changing, particularly in regard to *Wigoleis*.[7] In contrast, in 1971, Alois Brandstetter argued that *Wigoleis* should not be judged as deficient, but rather perceived as a creative reworking and classic representative of Early New High German prose novels (Brandstetter 1971, 21–24). In this chapter, I unveil a distinct agenda for the under-researched *Wigoleis* adaptation through a closer look at how its female roles are constructed in text and paratext, both as an individual act of creation and as an adaptation of *Wigalois*. Uncovering the ways in which themes from *Wigalois* are continued and adapted cements *Wigoleis'* position as an act of early modern reception of Wirnt's romance. The supplementary discussion of the illustrations in *Wigoleis* enables us to expand our studies into transmedial adaptations. My approach demonstrates that, in Mary, the "translation" of Wirnt's concept of passivity and female devotion for an early modern audience culminates. Against the backdrop of Mary as the ideal, the novel's representation of female figures reveals a historic cultural and religious emphasis on the eve of the Reformation. As the Protestant movement began its separation from the Holy Catholic Church, the portrayal of female figures in *Wigoleis* conveyed an important extra-literary layer of discourse, which, as we will see, ensured the adaptation's success beyond denominational conflicts.

## 3.1 Mary's Divine Presence in *Wigoleis*

In *Wigoleis*, God's mother, Mary, plays a significant role from the very start. In the dedication preceding the story, the narrator draws on traditional topoi asking for God's and Mary's divine guidance and blessing for his project: "May God grant the work's successful conclusion. I set my hope in His divine grace and His kind mother that they will help me bring this work to a good end, as nobody is capable of achieving anything without their help." ("Got wöll das die [arbeit] såligklichen volpracht werde/ als ich in hoffnung seinen götlichen genaden/ vnd seiner lieben můter getrawe sie helffen mir dises werck zů eim gůtem ende bringen dann ye niemant on ir hilff nichtzen volbringen mag," *Wigoleis*, Aiiv). However, rather than simply being included as a figure of praise in the dedication as

---

does not focus on the audience but on the texts themselves (Müller 1985, 1–3). However, André Schnyder criticizes Müller's lack of focus on reception, for he sees these novels as objects that have to be understood with regards to both reception and production (Schnyder 2010, 21).

**7** See in particular, Jutta Eming's comparative analysis of the concept of the "Marvelous", and Judith Schönhoff's study of concepts of masculinity and femininity in early modern prose novels.

was common at the time, Mary's role remains significant throughout the adaptation. Moreover, as the narrator prays to her, Mary's identifying feature is not her virginity per se but her identity as Jesus' mother, a choice that sets the tone for the subsequent narration.

Like the narrator, Wigoleis repeatedly turns to Mary as recipient of his prayers, requesting the aid of both God (sometimes in the Trinitarian manifestation of Jesus, the son) and Mary throughout the narrative: "Lord, almighty God, I commend myself to you and your dear mother." ("Herr almechtiger gott/ ich beuilhe mich dir vnd deiner lieben můter," *Wigoleis*, Evr); "Lord Wigoleis thanked the almighty God and his honorable mother with all his heart." ("Herre Wigoleys [...] dancket dem almåchtigen gott vnnd seiner werden můtter Marie mit gantzem hertzen," *Wigoleis*, Hvr). In these cases, Mary's intervention serves the purpose of assuring either a successful tale told (for the narrator) or a successful quest (for Wigoleis). Mary's intercession serves a man who is pleading for her help. Mary is assumed to possess significant powers, enough to affect both the knight's and the narrator's endeavors. Yet, her significance and agency are tied to her maternal role. Both the narrator and Wigoleis address her with her maternality in mind. Her identity is defined via her son, the supposed Messiah. Addressing her as a mother represents a constant reminder that she is not, in herself, praiseworthy. It is only thanks to the fact that she is the Christian savior's mother that she gains relevance and ultimately power, bringing to her son the prayers she received.

Mary not only receives prayers but also informs the depiction of Wigoleis' mother, Florye. Already in Wirnt's *Wigalois*, mother and son share a special bond, contributing to her death from grief after she loses both Wigalois and her husband, Gawein. Both *Wigalois*' and *Wigoleis*' narrators portray the hero's mother as a courtly lady who insists on caring for the infant on her own: "Its [the child's] immaculate mother loved it so much that she [...] took care of it herself." ("sîn reiniu muoter woldez nie / von im gelâzen einen tac; / vor liebe si sîn selbe pflac," *Wigalois*, 1222–1225). The adjective "reiniu" [immaculate] already draws a parallel between the knight's mother and Mother Mary, a loose association that the *Wigoleis* narrator expands through the motif of breastfeeding: "Because of the great love she felt for her son, she would not entrust him to a wet nurse, but rather raised him by herself and fed him with her (little) breasts, as she did deliberately and wholeheartedly." ("Die kunigin aber durch der grossen liebe willen so sie zů irem sůn hete/ wolt sie den kainer ammen beuelhen/ sunder den selbs ziehen/ vnd mit iren brüstlin erneren/ als sie dann mit hôchstem fleiß vnd grossem ernst volbracht." *Wigoleis*, Aviiiv). It was uncommon for courtly ladies and noblewomen to breastfeed children themselves in the Middle Ages as well as in the early modern period, in contrast to the lower classes, because regular breastfeeding would distract a noble lady from her duties and thus was passed on to an appointment female. As a consequence, both domestic and institutional wet-nursing among nobility was common and became "the most remunerative of women's unskilled labor" (Sperling 2013, 9). Royal queens who breastfeed are scarce in MHG literature, but examples can be found in *Wigalois* as well as Wolfram's *Parzival* and Ulrich von Zatzikhoven's *Lanzelet*. In all three cases, the iconographic reference is Mary nursing her infant son. The image of *Maria lactans* [nursing Mary] as nursing mother was already well established in Europe at the beginning of the twelfth century, and such images continued to circulate with broad popularity through at least 1500 (Wenzel 1996, 222). By tying Florye's breastfeeding to Mariological iconography, the *Wigoleis* author utilizes the popularity of this image for his own purposes.

But already prior to the text's evocation of Florye nursing her infant son, the framework for a Mariological interpretation of *Wigoleis* is established when the narrator informs the audience, "when the time came for her to have a child, she gave birth to as beautiful a son as one could have wished for. Thus, all the people in the whole country rejoiced." ("als ir zeyt kam das sie geberen solte/ gebar sie ainen schönen sůn nach wunnsch gestalte/ des sich alles volck in dem gantzen land was erfreüwen," *Wigoleis*, Aviiiv). Luther's 1522 translation of the New Testament from Greek into German (the so-called September Testament) is, of course, too late to inform this moment, but earlier translations into German included similar phrasing, some of which were printed in Augsburg and Strasbourg, the locations of the first and second *Wigoleis* printings. In close proximity to such translations, that *Wigoleis* would present the birth of a son as cause for a whole kingdom to rejoice indicates a strong messianic connection.[8] The hero Wigoleis, presented as a good Christian who opposes witchcraft and magic, grows up to fight against an enemy well-versed in dark arts and eventually brings salvation to an enchanted kingdom and its inhabitants.

Besides her breastfeeding, the text emphasizes Florye's almost heavenly features: "Lord Gabon was welcomed well and received amicably by the beautiful Florye, the sister of the king. When he looked upon her, he thought he'd seen an angel rather than a human." ("Herr Gabon ward da gar schone empfangen mit freüntlichem umbfahen von der schönen Florye des küngs schwester/ als er die ansahe beducht in nit einen menschen/ befunder [sic!] einen engel gesehen," *Wigoleis*, Aviiiv). Yet, Florye is not predominantly praised for her angelic beauty, but rather for her role in facilitating her son's quest and upcoming

---

[8] I agree here with Schönhoff, who bases her similar impression on the so-called *Mentelin Bibel* (1466) (Schönhoff 2008, 66).

tasks. Both Florye and Mary contribute to their children's messianic perception by being of flawless character and constitution, something perceived as impacting their sons' good characters, and, simultaneously, they only merit praise because of their sons' messianic identities.[9] One cannot help but be reminded of Wirnt's emphasis on female devotion as tied to a male counterpart. Here, the male counterpart has become the son, ennobling and upgrading the perception and value of the mother.

And, just like in Wigalois, the consequences of the male object of devotion's disappearance are the same; *Wigoleis*' Florye dies of a broken heart upon the loss of her husband and son, which is only briefly addressed by a messenger at the end of the narrative: "The messenger sighed and cried and said: My Lord, as God wills, she is unfortunately dead from longing for you and your friend [Gabon]." ("der bot erseüfftzet vnd ward seer záheren vnd sprach. Herr wie gott will die ist leyder todt vor grosser klag nach eüch vnnd eüeren ameys." *Wigoleis*, Kiir). Her briefly-mentioned death concludes her fate, underscoring that her life served primarily as a vessel for the arrival of the messianic hero, Wigoleis; thus, her portrayal helps establish the hero as the chosen one.

But why Mary? As Bridget Heal (2007) explains in her study *The Cult of Virgin Mary in Early Modern Germany*, Mary was omnipresent to a contemporary audience: "In 1500 a visitor to any German town or city would [...] have encountered numerous manifestations of Marian piety." (Heal 2007, 2). Most churches had at least one altar dedicated to Mary (Heal 2007, 1). The impact of the emerging Protestant Reformation made no difference to this particular iconography. Despite general polemics targeting the cult of Mary, Mary remained a role model regarding faith and an important witness to the life of Christ for Martin Luther (1483–1546) and Huldrych Zwingli (1484–1531). Only with the next generation of reformers does this phenomenon begin to change. John Calvin's (1509–1564) battle against idolatry, for instance, leads him to condemn all remnants of medieval Marian devotion while he simultaneously praises the historic Mary for her faith, which even God honored by making her the mother of Christ (Heal 2007, 4–5). Despite the reformers' general resentment of Marian idolatry and pilgrimages to Marian shrines, the extremism of radical reformers and the wish to reach a

---

[9] The interpretation of *Wigalois* as a messianic or at least saint-like figure is further developed in Ulrich Füetrer's *Wigalois* adaptation in *Buch der Abenteuer*. Here, one of the cursed knights of Korntin requests intercessional prayer from Wigalois, perceiving his saintliness: "Pray for us diligently so that our pain, and hardship, and current lives may change." ("Pitt got fur vnns mit vleisse, / das sich wenndt vnnser not, / dy pein vnnd vnnser weysse!" *Wigoleis* 170).

broad audience led even this major group of moderate reformers to defend some Marian beliefs of non-biblical origins (Heal 2007, 5; Rubin 2009, 255).[10]

Therefore, the extensive reworking of *Wigoleis* in 1519 required no changes in regard to Mariological references and motifs in order to appeal to an audience beyond the great Christian schism of the sixteenth century. In her monograph *Mother of God: A History of the Virgin Mary* (2009), Miri Rubin argues that the Protestant incorporation actually led to an increase in Mariology throughout the sixteenth century: "In these decades Mary achieved the highest levels of visibility and availability, her images not only sculptured and painted and carved, but also reproduced in prints, engravings and woodcuts that were cheap and soon ubiquitous too" (Rubin 2009, 355). *Wigoleis vom Rade* bears witness to an early modern audience's fascination with Mary by including her so heavily in the adaptation. Mary represents, in her faithfulness and dedication to her son, a significant role model for both female *and* male contemporary audiences. Mary models a pious devotion to Christ, serving as an inspiration for contemporaneous Christians of all denominations. *Wigoleis'* emphasis on Mariological imagery proves successful, leading to at least five subsequent editions later in the sixteenth century (Weidenmüller 1910, 2).

*Wigoleis'* emphasis on Mary, the most celebrated female biblical figure, is part of a strong Christian reconstruction already evident in the 1493 adaptation. Even more than in *Wigalois*, Christian piety contrasts with evil forces, "heathens" who employ dark magic and pray to a syncretistic multitude of deities. The text considers all magic elements evil; as Eming has argued, this feature points towards a sixteenth century radical turn against magic, at least within religious and juridical institutional and literary conventions (Eming 1999, 267). Where *Wigalois* offered a complex moral framework of knightly honor for men and *triuwe* for female figures, protagonists in *Wigoleis* tend to be either entirely good or bad. This reinforced division creates a strong demarcation between the figures. "Heathen" knights or courtly ladies are not evaluated based on their adherence to courtly standards, but instead based only on their religious devotional practices. In consequence, the author of *Wigoleis* represents Roaz (here: Roas) as an evil magician counting on the constant support of his demonic entourage ("hoelwicht") to which he consigned his soul (*Wigoleis*, Giiiiv). Portraying the opponent of the main hero as evil underscores *Wigoleis'* tendency to rely on black-and-white narrative devices, omitting potential ambiguity within the description of figures and scenes entirely. Roas acts out of "evil cunning" and "sorcery"

---

**10** Georg Söll emphasizes that the early reformers retained more Catholic Mariology than later generations, albeit with a stronger focus on biblical accounts of Mary (Söll 1984, 193–194).

("bösse listigkeit" and "zauberey", both *Wigoleis*, Aviiiv); Wigoleis is marked, by contrast, as a good Christian, acting from a place of trust in God's and Mary's guidance.

The demonization and moral devaluation of non-Christian characters becomes best visible in the case of Roas' wife Laneyt. In *Wigalois*, the concept of *triuwe* informs the representation of female figures across religious-cultural boundaries.[11] The *Wigoleis* adaptor eliminates the topic almost entirely and, as a consequence, re-erects these boundaries. Roas' wife is not only portrayed vaguely as "heathen"; she actively requests the support of a variety of non-Christian deities including Mohamed and Apollo, recipients of her supplicant prayers, as well. Nevertheless, she dies as a consequence of her devotion and due to a broken heart over the loss of her husband, whom *Wigoleis* defeats by inflicting fatal wounds. The narrator points out explicitly that, despite her clearly identifiable *triuwe*, Laneyt cannot be saved: "I bemoan forever that such a devoted woman had never been baptized." ("das einn soliches getreües weib nit mit dem tauff soli begossen sein. das mů ß mich immer reüwen." *Wigoleis*, Hiir). Not devotion but baptism is the relevant feature for salvation in this adaptation, and Laneyt is missing it. The narrator's lamentation of Laneyt's position – devoted to her husband, yet unsaved – demonstrates the text's clear distinction between Christians and non-Christians. This distinction correlates with *Wigoleis'* introduction of Mary as role model for devoutly Christian women. Unlike the narrator and the Arthurian knight, Laneyt does not turn to Mary for support; instead, she invokes a myriad of deities. The recipients of one's prayers guide the audience in their interpretation – helping to decipher which characters are good and bad. With this enhancing of contrasts, the author of *Wigoleis* forgoes the possibility of enhancing the portrayal of female figures under the overarching theme of *triuwe*. In the process of adaptation, the conflicted portrayal of women in *Wigalois* is solved in favor of a simplified model for the new audience.

Laneyt is devaluated within this newly applied moral framework, and consequently her tomb's grandeur is only mentioned in passing:

> The virgins took the Lady Laneyt, who had lost her life out of great love and faithful constancy, and brought her to the grave. This grave was adorned with such riches of beautiful gemstones and gold that it would be a wonder to tell of. I will refrain from doing so for brevity, [and also] because such treasures and riches are incredible for us. Furthermore, such an excursion is pointless and would only lengthen the tale.

---

[11] As Schönhoff has argued convincingly, *Wigoleis* reflects the loss of a meaningful *minne* discourse, which affects especially the portrayal of female figures in the adaptation (Schönhoff 2008, 225–227).

("di iunckfrawen [...] namen die frawen Laneyt die durch groß lieb und ståte treüe ir leben verloren hat vnd brachten die zů dem grab wölliches grab mit sölicher grosser reycheyt von edlem gesteyne vnnd gold gezieret was das wunder dauon zůsagen wr. das laß ich durch kürtze vnderwegen. dann söllich groß kost vnd reychtumb bey vnns gantz ungeleublich sinnd. auch an söllicher sag nitt mer vil ligtt den das die hystori dardurch gelengert würde." *Wigoleis*, Hiir–Hiiv).

Her *triuwe* is mentioned, but since the concept receives no elaboration in *Wigoleis*, this is of little significance. The marvelous riches of her tomb and the multimedia communication of her devotion that, in *Wigalois*, made her tomb a memorial for *triuwe* are dismissed with the brief remark that the audience could not believe the stunning riches anyways. As the narrator explains, any further discussion of her tomb would be "pointless," as it would prolong the narrative unnecessarily. Considering that the *triuwe* concept loses its significance, Laneyt's portrayal as female character misguided in religious devotion makes her an anti-role model for the audience, directly contrasting with the ideal of Mary as embodied by Florye.

## 3.2 Female Victimhood and Transgression

Although many early modern authors were concerned with heterosexual matrimonial relationships (including the qualities necessary to lead a pious household), and biblical heroines were increasingly on display in sixteenth century literature, the adaptor of *Wigoleis* takes a different path.[12] The adaptation, as Dreeßen, Eming, and Melzer similarly argue, displays no interest in love relationships or marriage (Eming 1999, 253, 269–270; Dreeßen 1994, 92; Melzer 1972, 102). Such unanimous scholarly agreement indicates that this may be a noteworthy feature of *Wigoleis*, not necessarily a consequence of a shift in literary aesthetics and conventions. Indeed, other Early New High German prose novels of the time provide female figures with greater agency within the realm of love and heterosexual partnerships, including *Magelone* (1470, edited by Veit Warbeck 1527), *Melusine* (adapted by Thüring von Ringoltingen 1456), and even *Fortunatus* (1509). By contrast, female figures are even more instrumentalized to the hero's journey in *Wigoleis* than in Wirnt's *Wigalois*. I argue, however, that this feature results directly from engagement with the Wigalois tradition and the focus on idealized femininity. Already in *Wigalois*, love and marriage are not

---

12 Early Humanist marriage and household treatises were popular and widespread genres of the period. See among many others Bennewitz 1996; Dallapiaza 1983.

essential features nor foci of the text, in contrast to Hartmann von Aue's *Erec* or Iwein and Chrétien's earlier treatment of the material. That Mariological motherhood and adoration, and bearing witness to a knight's success are the only roles available for the female figures of *Wigoleis* is a direct result of the adaptational interpretation of the MHG predecessor. They are otherwise portrayed as thoroughly dependent on men, especially for knightly protection.

This logic informs the Stone of Virtue scene, which in *Wigoleis* expands the topic of knightly responsibility. Gabon's (*Wigalois:* Gawein) behavior against a woman is mentioned once again, with specifics:

> The very stone's nature was such that nobody who was not perfectly virtuous was able to touch it. And although there were many famous and virtuous knights at the Round Table, none of them was able to come closer than six feet. Only King Arthur sat on it. Lord Gabon could reach it with his hand but no further. He missed his opportunity to sit on the stone when he embraced a virgin against her will. Therefore, he had to be punished by a non-rational creature such as the stone named Florant.

> ("Der selbe stein was einer solicher art/ das den niemant dorffte berůren/ dann die volkommenlich all tugendt an in hetten. Vnd wie vil tugentlicher hochberůmpter ritter bey der tafelrunde waren/ so mocht doch keiner nåher/ dann einer klaffter weite zů im genahen/ on allein künig Artus saß darauff. Herr gabon reichet mit der handt dar/ vnd nit nåher. Das der sitzes auff dem stein entberen můste/ verworcht er/ das er eines mals ein iunckfrauwen über iren willen umbfieng/ darumb můst er von einer vnuernünfftigen creatnr [sic!][13]/ als von dem stein Florant genant/ gestrafft [...] werden." *Wigoleis*, Biv)

Gabon embraced a maiden against her will ("umbfieng"), a clear violation of courtly, refined manners (Melzer 1972, 50). For this misbehavior, Gabon deserves to be punished, in this case by the stone called Florant. This measure described as an active deed by the stone refers to the fact that Gabon cannot sit on the stone, compared to Arthur and Wigoleis who do so thanks to their flawless characters. The stone thus becomes an anthropomorphized judge of character. Even this non-rational, non-sentient being, as the narrator points out, is capable of identifying Gabon's behavior as misconduct – a behavior that looks even worse considering that a woman is supposed to be the knight's ward. In the context of idealizing the devoted, passive women, knightly protection granting safety is paramount.

A longer passage following this episode emphasizes Gabon's guilt in the context of general sexual assault:

---

**13** The u/n transposition was, however, common in early modern typesetting.

## 3.2 Female Victimhood and Transgression — 43

O, if these wicked, stupid idiots, who not only embrace virgins against their will but also rape them, would now be punished according to the seriousness of their guilt – I believe they all would lose their heads! But, unfortunately, no punishment remains when those who should issue a judgment are the very ones who would most of all deserve it.

("O solten jetz die freflen ŏden tŏrper/ die iunckfrauwen über iren willen/ nicht allein umbfahen/ sunder(?) auch freuelichen gewaltigen gestrafft werden nach grŏsse der schuld/ ich gelaub ir wurden on zal die hăupter verlieren. Aber es ist leider alle straff auß/ wann die soliches solten straffen/ die verschulden selbs aller meist." *Wigoleis*, Biir).

The narrator laments that men are not prosecuted for misconduct against women due to the corruption of the authorities. However, even though the text heavily criticizes violence against women and does not attempt to exonerate Gabon in contrast to *Wigalois*, misconduct against a woman is used as a pretext for discourse on justice and the juridical system. The woman remains name- and identity-less in this scene – a scene in which even a stone receives a name and character traits – underscoring her irrelevance, her status as a mere tool to instigate a debate.

The giants' attempted rape of a virgin, the second instance of sexual violence against a female character in *Wigalois*, is featured in this adaptation too. As in *Wigalois*, this scene of attempted rape retains its focus on the knight's actions rather than the woman's suffering, with its description remaining very similar to Wirnt's text: "Then he [Wigoleis] saw a virgin sitting in a meadow gesturing heartrendingly and defending herself vehemently. Two strong giants were sitting with her. They wanted to take her virginity by force." ("do sahe er [Wigoleis] ein iunckfrawen sitzen anff [sic!] einer wisen/ klåglichen gebåren vnd sich starck weren. Bey ir sassen zwen starck risen/ die wolten sie mågtlicher keüsch enteret haben." *Wigoleis*, Bvir). Wigoleis immediately identifies a damsel-in-distress scenario and picks a fight with the giants, which he wins almost effortlessly.

Compared to *Wigalois*, the difference in this scene lies in a dwarf's covert witnessing of the attempted rape and reporting it to the messenger maiden, who is then sent initially to the Arthurian court in order to find a knight capable of liberating her queen's enchanted country: "The dwarf had secretly been following the knight to watch his deeds. He went to the [messenger] maiden and told her all what he had seen." ("Nůn was das zwerglin dem ritter heimlichen nachgegangen zů sehen sein getate/ das gieng zů der iungfrauwen vnnd saget ir alles das er gesehen hette." *Wigoleis*, Bvir). The dwarf displays *curiositas* [curiosity/ desire for knowledge], the urge to see and witness the world and its marvels in order to understand it – a central theme, for example, in other Early New High German prose texts such as *Fortunatus* (1509) as well as the *Historia von D.*

*Johann Fausten* (1578). In *Wigoleis*, the witness guarantees that an audience perceives the knight's deeds. The dwarf as witness-within emphasizes the status of the hero as a capable knight who, unlike his father, lives up to his knightly, masculine responsibility in light of the damsel-in-distress scenario. Hence, masculine heroism is contingent on female victimhood, just as female passivity depends on masculine heroism.

The dwarf witnessing this scene fulfills a second function: he recognizes the skills of the Arthurian hero despite Wigoleis' youth. He is portrayed as a trustworthy judge of the hero' skills who models proper behavior towards the young knight for the messenger maiden. Repeatedly, the messenger maiden expresses frustration with Wigoleis. His task, in her eyes, is to liberate her country, a task she does not believe the young knight would manage to accomplish. The scenario with the damsel and giants illustrates, as in *Wigalois*, that the messenger maiden is mistaken in her underestimation of Wigoleis' knightly aptitude. The dwarf is there to point out her lack of judgment and negative attitude toward the young knight: "The dwarf strongly disapproved of such a proud reply." ("Dem Zwerglin mißuiel solich stoltze antwurt gar sere." *Wigoleis*, Bvr) or "The Dwarf was displeased and said: You act unjustly." ("Dz zwerglin ward unmůtig vn*d* sprach [...] ir hůt [sic!] aber vnrecht [...]." *Wigoleis*, Bvir). Correcting the messenger maiden multiple times, the dwarf demonstrates that, according to the text's internal hierarchy, this uncourtly creature ranks higher than she does. Thus, despite being the character that brings an Arthurian knight to (successfully) help her country, the messenger maiden is marked as deficient, one who shows no empathy toward a woman in distress nor the text's would-be hero. She cannot see Wigoleis' true value, something even a dwarf is capable of recognizing. This is an additional form in which female figures depend on male figures, in this case to receive guidance in interpreting events and perceiving reality "correctly".

In contrast with damsels-in-distress and angelically passive mothers, female figures who seize agency play a reduced role in *Wigoleis*; the Amazon Marine and the wild woman Ruel demonstrate this minimization as a consequence of the author's adaptational decision to simplify the portrayal of female figures. Ruel, an uncourtly woman who lives in the woods, exists solely as a representation of the transgressive potential of female figures' agency. The narrator of *Wigoleis* strips her portrayal of the comedic elements featured in *Wigalois*, elements grounded in intertextual references to courtly ladies from other MHG romances and a discourse of sexual inversion (i.e. Ruel's attempts to sexually dominate the hero). The *Wigoleis* narrator presents Ruel only as a badly behaving woman, contrasting directly with Mary, the text's female role model. What remains in *Wigoleis*' depiction of the encounter between Wigoleis and Ruel is an illustration of the

## 3.2 Female Victimhood and Transgression — 45

hero's correct knightly behavior – his refusal to draw a sword against a woman – and the motivation for her violence, revenge for the murder of her husband ("There once was a king named Floyr of Belandt. This very king slayed her beloved husband named Feros without cause and threw his corpse into the lake, which was a very un-chivalrous deed." ["Es was ein künig mit name*n* geheissen Floyr von belandt der selbig künig erschlůg onschuld ire*n* lieben man geheissen Feros vn*d* warff den also toden in den see/ das doch vast vnritterliche getha*n* was."] *Wigoleis*, Fiiv). Yet, the justice of her actions is diminished as the narrator points out that she explicitly mistakes Wigoleis for the king who killed her husband: "She assumed he was this very Floyr himself [...]. In order to revenge her beloved husband, she attacked him with guile and without any warning." ("Nun vermeinte sy es wer der selb Floyr/ [...] ire*n* lieben man rechen griff sy in vnrŏdlichen vn*d* vngewarnet an," *Wigoleis*, Fiiv). Not only does Ruel attack Wigoleis erroneously, but the narrator also describes her actions explicitly as dishonorable ("unroedlichen"). The case of the wild woman underscores the text's presentation of a black-and-white portrayal of women, focused on the dangers of female figures' agency. Active female figures are condemned as morally transgressive and as acting based on flawed reasoning. Passive female figures are, in contrast, admired and idealized.

Of the transgressive female figures featured in *Wigoleis*, Ruel receives more attention than the Amazon Marine (here: Marene), who embodies the seemingly contradictory depiction of female figures in *Wigalois* through her hybrid identity as fascinating female warrior and unmaidenly maiden. Here, in contrast with her portrayal in *Wigalois*, Marene is a solitary Amazon, deprived of her companions. Marene appears as a singular figure and is mentioned only briefly due to the almost unbelievable nature of her actions (rather than due to her performance of *triuwe*, as with other female figures of the Wigalois universe): "But we should not forget the manly deed of the royal virgin named Marene, who achieved unheard-of, marvelous deeds." ("yedoch sollen wir auch in besunder nit vergessen der manlichen gethatt der küniglichen magt genent Marene die vachte mitt streyt sŏlliche wünder das es vngeleüblich ist." *Wigoleis*, Kivf). The emphasis on manly acts as "unheard-of, marvelous deeds" hints at a transgression with which the *Wigoleis* narrator refuses to engage. Rather than exploring the transgression caused by female agency as *Wigalois* does (despite, of course, that such female figures are either ridiculed or killed), *Wigoleis* presents a text that dismisses the potential at the outset. Indeed, immediately after the narrator introduces Marene to the audience, she is killed by a Turkish fighter (*Wigoleis*, Kiir). That Marene's presence is so drastically reduced in the narrative reflects the clear adaptational choice made by the *Wigoleis* adaptor: to maintain an overall focus on Wigoleis, the male knight, and dramatically relegate female figures to the background.

## 3.3 Aesthetics of Passivity

Thus far, we have explored several tendencies of the *Wigoleis* adaptation, including its emphasis on Mariological iconography, the need for witnesses to validate a male's knightly aptitude, and reduced active female roles in comparison to *Wigalois*. Such features are not only found in *Wigoleis'* written text but are visible in the woodcuts accompanying the narrative as well. Since *Wigoleis* was conceptualized as a text-image publication, the images offer important insight into the adaptation's reception, interpretation, and success. By the time this work was conceived, images were established as an essential part of the Wigalois tradition. Adaptations have included pictorial material from the fourteenth through the twenty-first centuries, appearing in forms as various as murals, illuminated codices, woodcut-illustrated books and even a graphic novel. Prominent representatives of this pictorial tradition include the Leiden Codex (LTK 537, 1372); murals at Castel Runkelstein (Southern Tyrol, commissioned around 1390); the Donaueschingen Codex (Ms. 71, ca. 1416–1421); the woodcut-illustrated *Wigoleis vom Rade* (1493/1519)[14]; a modern translation of *Wigoleis* (1841), partially illustrated by Ludwig Richter; and the graphic novel *Die Phantastischen Abenteuer des Glücksritters Wigalois* [*The Fantastic Adventures of Wigalois, Knight of Fortune*] (2011). In general, the image-program of the illustrated *Wigalois* adaptations sees a significant reduction in motifs found in the texts, offering mainly a story of one heroic knight at the expense of accompanying and secondary narratives.

The images in *Wigoleis* are still very much indebted to a medieval tradition in which text and image are often used together to communicate the narrative (Wenzel 1995, 301). The complete print includes 35 black-and-white woodcuts, each preceded by a *titulus*, an early form of chapter titling.[15] The evenly distributed woodcuts (one every two or three pages) provide structure for the narrative,

---

**14** Gotthard Oswald Marbach's *Wigalais vom Rade* (1841) is a loose modern translation of the 1519 text, being the eighteenth volume in his extensive anthology of German "Volksbücher." Richter contributed several of the images that represent an idealized-idyllic Middle Ages, as was typical of the time. Of the seven illustrations accompanying the text, three are attributed to Richter (albeit executed by a xylographer).

**15** I ground the remainder of this chapter in the discussion of images included with the 1519 printing of *Wigoleis*, not the 1493 printing, of which several pages are missing.

though not all illustrations correspond with the text. *Wigoleis*, thus, was conceived as a text with an elaborate image program, which, as we will see in this section, underscores our previous findings about the portrayal of female figures.¹⁶ The evidence suggests that, indeed, these images were meant to communicate the same message by means of pictorial narration. The illustrations in early printed books were primarily included in order to sell books (Ader 2010, 8, 17). To make these pre-modern books profitable, printing blocks were often reused for other book projects (already in Kristeller 1888, 1). In the case of *Wigoleis*, all the illustrations adhere to the same style, and illustrations that feature motifs special to the Wigalois universe, such as the Wheel of Fortune and the Stone of Virtue, indicate that at least some of the woodcuts were produced exclusively for the *Wigoleis* edition from 1493 and subsequently 1519.¹⁷ The fact that the majority of woodcuts in *Wigoleis* were made for this specific narrative underscores the relevance of the iconographic program for this adaptation. The iconographic program and specific images of the 1519 edition repeat that of the 1493 edition, which reinforces this impression. The images solidify the adapation's interpretation of female figures and translate the increased female inactivity and their core role as witnesses to knightly heroism into the pictures.

The importance of these images is echoed in scholarship. In his monograph *Imagining the Text: Ekphrasis and Envisioning Courtly Identity in Wirnt von Gravenberg's "Wigalois"* (2016) and in other different essays, James H. Brown centers his analysis of *Wigalois* and its pictorial adaptations around the theoretical framework of *ekphrasis* or verbal descriptions of visual representations.¹⁸ By contrast, Andrea Grafetstätter explores solely visual material and uncovers changes in the pictorial representation of the narrative, comparing the Donaueschingen codex to the print from 1493 (and to some extent to the 1519 edition). Grafetstätter (2013, 383) concludes that within these adaptations female figures are mostly placed in limited architectural (safe) spaces or in the company of other female figures. Female figures, according to Grafetstätter, are positioned

---

**16** Once the printing of wood block and letterpress type in a single frame was technically mastered, the woodcut became the leading medium for illustrations (Laube 2004, 47). Classen argues that the illustrations in the early modern prose novels were included for a potentially low-literacy readership, extending the relevance of Pope Gregory's earlier argument that images are meant to convey the respective stories for the illiterate (Classen 1995, 66).
**17** On the use of generic in contrast to specific illustrations, see van D'Elden 2012, 282. According to van D'Elden, in unspecified scenes, a knight would never be directly identified; only the context provided in the illustration enables such an identification (van D'Elden 2012, 263, 269–270, 282).
**18** Emphasizing both the written word and visual imagery, Brown writes in the tradition of scholars such as Horst Wenzel and Kathryn Starkey.

in groups and are placed only within confined buildings that seem to frame them but actually restrict their movement. Architecture offers a protection and, thus, underscores the lack of agency in the same way their need for male, knightly protection does. Based on the previous analysis, I argue that these images do not represent merely an illustrator's ideology but significantly underscore the point communicated in the printed text.

Key aspects of the text's illustrations are not only a result of changes in the narrative itself but also of changes in contemporaneous visual aesthetics. Unlike earlier pictorial adaptations, such as the Leiden Codex, a changing attitude towards experiencing and witnessing culture is "translated" into the illustrations through the inclusion of figures of witnesses. Witnesses of the plot are placed in front of walls, looking over walls, and peering out of windows in a variety of scenes.[19] For example, while the text explains that Wigoleis sat on the Stone of Virtue, the image and *titulus* present Wigoleis *standing* on the stone, elevated on a pedestal, observed by king and queen, with the latter placed behind the former within a doorframe. The inclusion of the queen represents an increase in female witnesses. As such, the queen witnesses Wigoleis succeeding in the initial character test, being able to sit on the Stone of Virtue. In other woodcuts, female figures are inserted as spectators for knightly combats. One representative example, used twice in the text, displays two knights on horses facing each other with erected lances. One of them is marked though his code-of-arms as Wigoleis. The background shows a tent in the right half of the image; two female figures dressed in courtly fashion peek from behind the tent and observe the fight. Similar to the queen, they become witnesses to knightly combat and ultimately to Wigoleis' success. All these figures, marked by their clothing and regalia as possessing courtliness, stand in for the large majority of the audience to knightly combat. Their presence is even more significant as they are placed in the framework of courtliness, which reflects on a hero worthy of their presence and admiration.

In general, female figures, often in groups, are depicted witnessing heroic deeds, or, as Grafetstätter has proposed, in moments of arrival or departure, thus in a constant posture of passively awaiting the knight (Grafetstätter 2013, 386). Their position of immobility, as passive witnesses, sharply contrasts with the role filled by actively fighting knights and thus reinforces that they serve the hero in his heroism and knightly deeds. The figure established as a core wit-

---

**19** According to the *titulus*, one image depicts a knight sitting on the stone, when in the picture he is in fact standing next to it (Avr). This latter depiction, however, corresponds with the one from Leiden Codex.

ness to Wigoleis' deeds in the verbal representation of the text, the dwarf, is portrayed as a female dwarf in a dress, her hair tied up into buns, whenever included in an image (*Wigoleis*, Biiiv, Dir). The illustrations underscore the impression given in the written part of the narrative: female figures' core function is to admire the knight and witness, in particular, Wigoleis' heroism. The woodcuts of the female dwarf mirror and exaggerate this impression, turning the central witness of the knight's actions into a woman.

Two female figures deviate from *Wigoleis*' iconographic program of female figures as witnesses: Lady Beleare (here unnamed) and Ruel. Lady Beleare is depicted bringing a garment to the naked hero in the forest; the specifics of this scene indicate that this is a woodcut purposely made for *Wigoleis*. Grafetstätter has argued convincingly that this image draws on an iconographical trope present in medieval images and religious plays: Mary providing Jesus with a cloth to cover his nakedness (Grafetstätter 2013, 390). Thus, the image emphasizes the text's Mariological theme and expands its representation via a second woman. As with Florye's depiction in the text, this image's reference to Mary draws on her identity as Christ's mother and, in consequence, parallels the male hero with the Messiah. The Mariological reference of the image, like that of the text, primarily serves Wigoleis' character development, underscoring that he is the chosen one and resembles the Messiah.

The second woman depicted as active is Ruel, the wild woman, portrayed in the moment when she fights the Arthurian knight. She is depicted naked, with flowing hair, a club in her right hand, leaping out of the cave towards the Arthurian knight and his horse. The image, in contrast to the written description, diminishes her unique physical features, retaining only her "boar's teeth" ("ein zan [...] gleich als einem eberschwein," *Wigoleis*, Fiir). Her uncourtly features, however, are underscored by her nakedness and long, flowing hair as well as her living in a cave. All the other female figures in the text are depicted wearing fine garments and with contemporary hairstyles. Further, Ruel no longer uses the hero's sword, as she does in the 1493 edition, but rather employs her own weapon, a club, which is often reserved for uncourtly figures such as giants in the MHG romances. This depiction further emphasizes her uncourtly features. Ruel is also portrayed in front of a specific architectural space, the cave, which underscores that all women are depicted within the protective frame of specific architectural spaces.[20] Although, the woodcut retains the feature of being depicted in front of a "protective space", it also marks Ruel clearly as a counterpart to the

---

**20** See also Grafetstätter 2013, 392.

other female figures portrayed in the woodcuts by emphasizing the uncourtliness of the space.

More than the protective architectural spaces, one structure in particular emphasizes the position of female figures: the tomb. Laneyt, Roas' wife, and Liamire, whose provocation initiates the epic battle at Namur, are both portrayed as corpses, each laid to rest in a rectangular memorial of architectural complexity with pillars and little towers in all four corners, connected by a tented roof that covers and protects each corpse. The same woodcut is used for both but with different *tituli*, both erroneously labeling the tomb as containing Wigoleis' future wife's corpse: "Here lies buried the beautiful Larie." ("hie ligt die schon Larie begraben," *Wigoleis*, Hiiiir), "Here lies buried Wigoleis' spouse." ("Hie littg [sic!] begraben herr wigoleys haußfrawe," *Wigoleis*, Iiiiv). Through their repetition and this wrongly attributed description, the tombs underscore the arbitrariness with which female figures are treated in the images, especially in the light of a specific and individually-marked hero. The repeated woodcuts of the tomb are the only images in which female figures appear alone. The tomb memorializes Laneyt and Liamire but simultaneously removes them from the world of the living. Moreover, by not including the figures of witness typically shown observing Wigoleis' brave deeds, the adaptation's audience members become the only mourners at these immortalized ladies' wake. The doubled tomb, I would argue, functions as the conclusive illustration of female passivity in *Wigoleis*. Female figures' most important role in the text is to witness knightly heroism; they themselves are deprived of figures of witness, emphasizing the key connection between being *seen* and being granted agency. The woodcuts grant witnesses to deeds performed by fully humanized men only. In their deaths, the female figures of *Wigoleis* are immortalized yet immobilized.

## 3.4 Conclusion

*Wigoleis* retains several central female figures from the MHG *Wigalois*; however, minor representational changes cause them to occupy an even more passive place in the adaptation than in Wirnt's text, offering a less conflicted representation as a consequence of the adaptational interpretation. The increased inactivity of female figures in *Wigoleis* is underscored by the portrayal of female figures' role as audience, as background to knightly success. Moreover, the text aestheticizes Mary, mother of Christ, as a role model for all women; both Wigoleis and the narrator pray to her, further emphasizing her idealized status. Yet such veneration turns Mary into a static object to be adored, with stasis being a crucial aspect of the Mariological iconography with which contemporaneous audiences were familiar. The text's focus on Mary's maternal, nurturing features additionally informs its portrayal of the most prominent mother figure in the narrative – Wigoleis' mother, Florye – and highlights the hero's messianic value. The focus on Mother Mary excludes non-Christian female characters from being admired like their Christian counterparts as well. The two essential and interconnected reworking tendencies in *Wigoleis* – the inclusion of Mother Mary as divine figure and the continued reduction of female figures' agency – serve the text's increased focus on the Arthurian knight. Female figures fade into the background and are only represented insofar as they serve the portrayal of a hero.

*Wigoleis* reflects interpretational choices made by the unknown author of the adaptation. As other fifteenth- and sixteenth-century prose romances demonstrate, these choices were not necessarily typical of early modern literature. In the early sixteenth century, on the eve of the Reformation, *Wigoleis'* construction of female figures conveyed an important extra-literary discourse and epitomized a cross-denominational fascination with Mary. Among Protestant and Catholic audiences, this focus on Mary ensured a broad reception of the text, leading to at least four subsequent editions in the sixteenth century alone (Weidenmüller 1910, 2). As discussed above, the female figures of *Wigoleis* were even more restricted in their agency than in *Wigalois*, which correlates with this historic situation. Women's spheres were much more restricted in the early modern period, and although the Reformation emphasized women's roles in the household, it restricted women even more than religious institutions in the preceding epoch (Kelly-Gadol 1977, 197; Wiesner 1998, 92). In addition, the separation between men's and women's work increased towards the early modern period. Nevertheless, love, marriage, and family are three core topics within religious and non-religious literary discourses of the time (Bachorski and Sciurie 1996, 11). *Wigoleis'* author does not engage with these fashionable topics but rather omits them altogether. This is, first and foremost, an adaptational choice, and not indicative of the early modern literary zeitgeist, which emphasized love, marriage, and family in distinctive ways. The author, instead, engages with contemporaneous popular beliefs primarily through the figure of Mary. By elevating her, and essentially informing the representation of all female figures in *Wigoleis* through this elevation, the adaptor renders ideal female figures as worthy of admiration only for *their* admiration of heroic knights. Therewith, in the process of adaption, *Wigalois'* connecting concept of devotion (*triuwe*) has been narrowed to admiration.

## 4 *Viduvilt:* Mothers Seizing Power

> And thereafter he came to regret that he did not wait for her counsel and that he did not go to her and hear her plea.
>
> ([un doz er ir rot nit beyt / doz wurd im dernokh leyd / un doz er nit zu ir kom / un' ir bet vernom], *Viduvilt*, 11r).[1]

With this brief comment, the narrator of *Viduvilt*, the first Yiddish adaptation of *Wigalois*, problematizes Gawein's refusal to listen to the concerns of his wife. He signals to the audience that Gawein (here: Gabein) made a consequential mistake: when Gabein's pregnant wife (here: Broktin) suggested that her husband take his magic belt with him to the Arthurian court, which would grant him re-entry to her realm, the knight refused. Gabein will regret this decision later, specifically by not being able to return to his wife to see his firstborn, Wigalois (here: Viduvilt), grow up. By contrast, the audience of the MHG *Wigalois* receives the following "advice" upon Wigalois' departure from his mother: "A wise man is not governed by a woman's advice." ("Swer sînen rât læt an diu wîp, dern ist ein wîser man." *Wigalois*, 1358–1359). Where *Wigalois* ridicules the mother's advice, the statement in *Viduvilt* holds the character's mother in much higher esteem, underscoring her wisdom. Throughout *Viduvilt*, other strong women join the knight's mother in earning high regard, particularly mothers who take their fate and that of whole countries into their own hands.

Both scenes from *Viduvilt*, despite minimal changes, are familiar scenarios that we have already encountered in *Wigalois* and *Wigoleis*: Gawein leaves his wife; in her husband's absence, she gives birth to the next-generation hero and raises him alone; later, the adult son leaves his mother, embarking on knightly quests and seeking his father; and the now son- and husband-less woman, grief-stricken, dies of a broken heart. The Yiddish adaptation includes most of these major plot points, signaling that it is likely just another retelling, albeit in a different language. In the portrayal of female figures, however, we find a major change: Viduvilt's mother does not die. Rather, at the end of the narra-

---

[1] All Yiddish quotes in this chapter appear in transliteration (by the author) and in English translation (by Jerold Frakes taken from his English *Viduvilt* translation: Frakes 2014, 184–237). I have used the YIVO transcription system, devised for Modern Yiddish, modifying it slightly, where appropriate, to represent Old Yiddish. The quotations are based on the manuscript held at Cambridge (Wren Library. MS F.12.44 [16th ct.]), supplemented by the Hamburg manuscripts (Hamburg, Staats- und Universitätsbibliothek, Cod. Hebr. 255 [16th ct.] and Cod. Hebr. 289 [16th ct.]) and Irving Linn's transliteration (Linn 1946) where passages in the codices are illegible (due to some ill-fated nineteenth and twentieth century attempts at preserving the material).

tive, she arranges a family reunion, something neither her husband nor her son managed to accomplish. As this chapter's epigraph indicates, the narrator establishes Viduvilt's mother early on as occasionally even wiser than her husband. Scholars who have regarded *Viduvilt* as outdated and deficient compared to Wirnt's *Wigalois*, a mere bad copy of a great original, have overlooked this important change (most notably Dreeßen 1994, 87). However, as this chapter shows, the Yiddish adaptation is a radical new retelling of the Arthurian knight's tale. With increased women's agency and other such "minor" changes being part of the narrative's overall reworking strategy, *Viduvilt* turns the story of Gawein's son into an Arthurian romance in which women are the power brokers.[2]

Both *Wigoleis* and *Viduvilt*, written within a century of each other, represent acts of creation and reception that approach the conflicted depiction of women in *Wigalois* with significant differences. Whereas *Wigoleis* adheres to the concept of devotion, *Viduvilt* continues the fascination with a broad range of active female figures without ultimately restricting their agency. *Viduvilt* provides its audience with far more empowered, complex women than those represented in previous Wigalois narratives. This change is not a mere inconsistency or consequence of a lack of understanding the source material; rather, these modifications represent the unknown adaptor's conscious choices. The adaptor drew on the tradition of adapting Arthurian romances as we have already seen in the preceding chapter, using the narrative model and structure of these texts in a very innovative and different way.

The Yiddish adaptation proved immensely popular. Three incomplete manuscripts[3] of *Viduvilt* exist – a high number for pre-modern Yiddish non-religious texts – dating from the sixteenth century and written in the so-called vaybertaytsh, a semi-cursive version of the Hebrew alphabet.[4] Scholars have argued that the narrative itself might be one or even two centuries older (Dreeßen 1994, 85; Jaeger 2000, 59). Unfortunately, the date, the adaptor's identity, and the place of composition remain unknown. Some sixteenth-century manuscripts point to Italy as the place of composition. During the period, Italy was a central location for the production of Yiddish literature. Later adaptations appear to

---

**2** The tendency to ascertain strong female roles continues in the later edition of *Viduvilt* by Josl of Witzenhausen, in which even more female figures receive names.
**3** Cod. hebr. 289 and 255, held at the Staats- und Universitätsbibliothek Hamburg, offer a mainly identical text, but cod. hebr. 255 consists only of a few leaves (*Viduvilt*. Hamburg, Staats- und Universitätsbibliothek, Cod. Hebr. 255 [16th ct.] and Cod. Hebr. 289 [16th ct.]).
**4** Sometimes used synonymously with máshkit (Katz 2015, 59).

have come from further north (Dreeßen 1994, 85; Jaeger 2000, 29).[5] Eventually, the Yiddish adaptation became a template for numerous reworkings, which indicates a fascination with the text among Yiddish-speaking audiences that would last for centuries. The most famous reworking presents *Artis Hof* by Joseph (Josl) ben Alexander Witzenhausen (Amsterdam 1671), which in a later print (Prague 1679) offers a thorough recasting in *ottava rima*, a popular Italian rhyme scheme.

Consisting only of roughly 4,200 verses, *Viduvilt* presents a much shorter version of the Wigalois narrative than previous iterations. Many scholars have argued that *Viduvilt* and *Wigalois* agree in terms of their plotlines (e. g. Cormeau 1978, 32; Howard 1972, 171);[6] primarily descriptions of clothing, fights, and festivities have been omitted in *Viduvilt*.[7] The most essential difference lies in the omission of the entire Namur episode, which, in *Wigalois*, takes place after the wedding festivities. In contraposition, *Viduvilt* concludes the narrative with the wedding itself. The elimination of the final epic Christian-versus-heathen battle illustrates the general abolishment of the concept of heathens in the Yiddish text. Not only is the fight between Roaz and Wigalois completely altered in the Yiddish text, Roaz is also not a "heathen" anymore. By focusing on the marriage of a royal couple and omitting the *chanson de geste* episode, the text seems at first glance to end with the classical climax of an Arthurian hero's career; this move appears to align itself more closely with the narratological tradition of Chrétien's romances, in which a *knight errant* acquires wife and kingdom through completing multiple quests.[8] However, a comparative analysis shows that the text's representation of women by no means offers a traditional take on the Arthurian genre.

The tendency of past scholarship to claim more-or-less similar plotlines between Wigalois narratives has obstructed a view of some significant changes and

---

[5] Yiddish literature had its first heyday in northern Italy between 1450/75 and 1600, a time that Erika Timm refers to as the first golden age of Yiddish literature (Timm 1991, 61).

[6] Häberlein argues that the Yiddish text largely kept the *histoire* of the narrative, with more extensive changes appearing only in the Roaz battle (Häberlein 2012, 70).

[7] Another major difference concerns the quest for the hero's father and the revelation of his identity as Gawein. Father and son recognize each other immediately in *Viduvilt*, therefore the whole question of Gawein's identity plays a much smaller role. The scene in which Viduvilt/Wigalois imagines an alternative life and questions his memories, for example, consists only of a couple of verses. The text's emphasis has shifted to something else entirely.

[8] Warnock uses this fact to reestablish a double cycle, claiming that the inexperienced *Viduvilt* gains a bride in the first cycle and then proves his heroic value ("'heldenhaften' Wert") in the second cycle (Warnock 1981, 152).

divergences.⁹ The majority of research on *Viduvilt* has been less interested in the function of the adaptation as a retelling of the story with a distinct agenda than in its "Jewish character."¹⁰ Most previous research has focused on finding religious motifs in order to reveal the Yiddish retelling of *Wigalois* simply as a Jewish adaptation of the earlier MHG text, intended for a Jewish audience.¹¹ For example, scholars have discussed the depiction of the enchanted Korntin in *Viduvilt* as representing concepts of the Jewish Biblical underworld, supposedly an implicit reference to Sheol and Gehenna (Jaeger 2000, 258, 288). The existence of a giant, although already present in the MHG text, supposedly refers to the fight between Moses and the giant Og, featured in the Talmud tractate *Berakoth* (Warnock 1981, 104; Tarantul 2002, 384–386); similarly, the hero's fight with a dragon has been tied to the Biblical Leviathan (Jaeger 2000, 269, 298). The search for Judaization within *Viduvilt* implies that a Jewish audience would not have found a courtly romance without explicitly Jewish references accessible or even interesting. The high number of *Viduvilt* adaptations and other Yiddish reworkings of non-religious material proves the opposite.¹²

By focusing mainly on uncovering explicitly Jewish elements in the text, scholars have overlooked many seemingly minor changes to *Viduvilt* and the subsequent implications of these differences. This focus represents a problematic endeavor that raises ongoing questions of whether some motifs from the Hebrew Bible could be regarded as Jewish-Christian, or only Jewish. One significant change that the majority of scholars have failed to explore adequately is the text's construction of female roles. *Viduvilt* cannot be judged as "deficient" for lacking elements of its Arthurian predecessors or reduced to a narrative focused

---

**9** Only Warnock acknowledges that both texts are very different in some regards, as he argues that the omission of the comments about morals and courtly ethics by the narrator and the omission of the final episode already change the general character of the work profoundly (Warnock 1981, 99).

**10** The most recent case in this context is Matthias Däumer's analysis of Witzenhausen's adaptation of the Yiddish *Viduvilt*. As Däumer sees it, many textual elements become indicators of a strong anti-Christian tone, from the name-giving and supposed baptism of the hero to the tree in which Viduvilt is captured (Däumer 2014, 267–268, 273–275).

**11** Cormeau, for example, sees the potential Jewishness of *Viduvilt* in its retaining of marvelous elements, many of which are also often found in rabbinical fables (Cormeau 1978, 40). Yet, he fails to support his claim with clear textual evidence from either *Viduvilt* or the mentioned fables. Margot B. Valles claims, "*Vidvilt* engages Jewish themes and values in so far as the poem adheres to religious and cultural principles that demand the separation of the divine from the realm of the foreign." (Valles 2013, 16).

**12** Yiddish adaptations of German non-religious material include Love and Adventure novels (*Floris- und Blanscheflor* and *Die schöne Magelone*), as well as heroic epics (*Dietrich von Bern, Meister Hildebrand, Siegenot*) and early modern prose novels (*Fortunatus*).

on finding a Jewish religious-cultural focus within the storyline. Rather, the adaptation experiments with possibilities of literature itself as fictional space, turning the text into a narrative within which women's agency is possible.[13] Wirnt's *Wigalois*, as representative of the Arthurian genre in general and its narratological structure in particular, was so well established by the time *Viduvilt* was conceived that the adaptor felt free to interpret the story in more unorthodox ways. What at first glance might seem contrary to the material and its literary tradition turns out to be the adaptor's productive approach to established models of medieval concepts of gender and marriage. The result is an Arthurian romance centered on women, especially mothers. The text harmonizes with earlier versions of the Wigalois narrative by connecting all women through a common theme but replaces the medieval concept of *triuwe* with the theme of motherhood. This extensive change in representation includes human as well as nonhuman figures, from the damsel-in-distress to the dragon – all of whom are now mothers. Acting within the interest of dynasty politics, the shifted focus on mothers appears to depict a matriarchal society.

In order to observe *Viduvilt*'s novel approach to representing women, we will explore their place within the nuclear family, particularly in regard to the politics of marriage. By the end of this chapter, it will become clear that the *Viduvilt* adaptor not only emphasizes women's agency, but also entirely reverses the gender roles commonly displayed in previous Wigalois narratives. This reversal, I argue, particularly diminishes the Arthurian knights Gabein and Viduvilt's impact and agency.

## 4.1 From Patriarchy to Matriarchy: Viduvilt's Name and Heritage

The most obvious change in this adaptation is the hero's name and consequently the adaptation's title. The German adaptations call Gawein's son Wigalois, Wigoleis, or other spelling variations; *Viduvilt* clearly alters this name more significantly. The Arthurian knight's name in Yiddish is the product of a misunderstanding, not from the adaptor but from a figure within the narrative. Before Gabein takes his leave to return to the Arthurian court, his pregnant wife asks him what to name their soon-to-be-born son, to which he answers: "Call him

---

[13] Astrid Lembke represents an exception, as her exploration of passivity and activity in *Wigalois* and *Viduvilt* puts both texts into dialogue beyond the Christian-Jewish debate (Lembke 2013).

whatever-you-want." ([Heys es vi du vilt], *Viduvilt*, 11r). The majority of scholars interpret these words as Gabein giving his wife the choice of what to name their child; they highlight how the soon-to-be mother literally mistakes Gabein's answer for a suggested name and calls their son accordingly: Vi-du-vilt.

The narrator does not comment on the misunderstanding, criticizing neither of Viduvilt's parents explicitly. Gabein's wife, however, has already been revealed as having more foresight than her husband, encouraging him to take the belt with him, a recommendation that Gabein disregards. Thus, the portrayal of the protagonist's father appears to highlight how the Arthurian knight takes little interest in the naming of his firstborn – a consequential sort of carelessness, for his hero-son is now blessed with a name that carries humorous traces rather than demanding respect. Asked about his name and identity, Viduvilt has to respond repeatedly with "as you wish." A trace of comic relief shimmers throughout the text whenever the hero's name is mentioned. The name change also carries a trace of arbitrariness, producing an ironic commentary on the importance of the messianic-like Arthurian hero we encounter in the other adaptations (especially in the nearly contemporary *Wigoleis*, whose narrative focuses on the central knight even more explicitly than in the MHG text).[14] The impression that Viduvilt is a weaker or less manly hero than his alter-egos from other adaptations reappears throughout the text, for he depends on many others to successfully complete his quests on his way to knighthood, kingdom, and marriage. The hero's name, a core feature of his identity, embodies this decrease in his agency and sets the stage for the unfolding Yiddish story.

Gabein misses the chance to give his son a proper knightly name. Later, another man in *Viduvilt* is deprived of the privilege to introduce the young knight to his knightly heritage. In *Wigalois*, and *Wigoleis* too, Gawein's son learns of his heritage from the bewitched king of Korntin (*Wigalois*, 4791–4813; *Wigoleis*, Eiiv) and is reunited with his father at the end of the romance. The quest for his father leads Wigalois to the Arthurian court, and the fact that Wigalois and Gawein do not know about their relationship until later creates significant suspense. In *Viduvilt*, this topic loses its significance.[15] Even before leaving his mother, the young knight learns everything about his heritage. After overhearing two men talking about Gabein being his father, Viduvilt confronts his mother, who subsequently familiarizes her son with his heritage. The young hero still travels to the Arthurian court to meet his father, but since they recognize each

---

14 See also Knaeble 2014, 86.
15 Dreeßen summarizes, "The new topic is genealogy rather than identity." ("Genealogie statt Identität ist also jetzt das Thema," Dreeßen 1994, 92).

other right away as father and son, the heritage aspect of the quest comes to an early conclusion.

Later, when the mother of Viduvilt's bride-to-be (here: Lorel the Fair) inquires after the Arthurian knight's heritage in order to ensure a marriage with good prospects for her daughter, Viduvilt willingly offers an extensive account of his lineage (*Viduvilt*, 43r–v).[16] Within that account, Viduvilt includes his maternal as well as his paternal heritage, emphasizing his noble lineage, as both of his parents were the descendants of kings. This account underscores the increased relevance of the maternal heritage, a heritage that is not only discussed with reference to the past but that informs the queen's character, as she is actively committed to shaping and ensuring a prosperous continuation of her family's lineage. Both Viduvilt's mother and his future mother-in-law are portrayed as significantly involved in the preservation of their pedigrees. In *Viduvilt*, genealogy thus becomes a field for the expression of powerful female figures.

## 4.2 Family Politics

Viduvilt's mother leads the charge of more active women in the Yiddish adaptation. Not only does she disclose knowledge of her son's ancestry, but she also ensures the preservation of her nuclear family, leading to their reunion at the end of the narrative. In *Wigalois* and *Wigoleis*, Wigalois and Gawein meet after the former' successful completion of his quest, becoming finally aware of their direct relationship. Nevertheless, the news that Gawein's wife, Wigalois' mother, died of a broken heart casts a shadow over their reunion. Having fulfilled her narrative duty to produce an heir and provide him with an extensive education, the mother figure is removed from these adaptations. Viduvilt's mother does not suffer the same fate. In contrast, rather than exhibiting heart-wrenching and eventually fatal grief over her losses, she steps into the background of the narrative momentarily only to reappear at the end, reuniting her family. Having received news of her son's wedding plans, she unceremoniously travels to attend the nuptials at King Arthur's court, where the family is finally reunited (*Viduvilt*, 81r–81v). It is the mother who achieves this reunion, something neither Viduvilt nor Gabein managed to accomplish.

---

[16] Viduvilt's pedigree is representative of the contemporaneous geopolitical reality. Melzer argues that *Viduvilt* is more about his heritage than his identity, which explains the queen's long inquiry (Melzer 1972, 92).

Viduvilt's mother, as it turns out, is not the only woman concerned with keeping the family together. The Yiddish adaptation increases the number of mothers featured in the text and strengthens their positions. This increase is achieved by transforming lovers or wives, characterized by *triuwe*, into mothers. In *Wigalois* and *Wigoleis*, for instance, the audience encounters the lady Beleare in the woods, mourning the abduction of her (male) partner, the object of her *triuwe*, by the dragon. In *Viduvilt*, the dragon robs her of both her husband and son (*Viduvilt*, 55r). In other words, the romantic loss is replaced by the loss of a whole family. After their reunion, the familial theme is emphasized even further: "They all three mounted the horse – for it was large and strong and noble – so that it could carry all three of them." ([oyf dos pferd zasn zi ale dray / ven es vos gros un shtark un fray.], *Viduvilt*, 58r). Riding away together on one horse, the little family leaves the scene, foreshadowing the comparable reunion of Viduvilt's family at the end of the text. Notably, the dragon itself is represented as being part of a family, as the audience learns later that Viduvilt kills not only the dragon but also its progeny.[17] Thus, the familial theme applies to all creatures of the narrative disregarding their representation as good or evil.

The text emphasizes the preservation and reunion of families but is also concerned with how families are initially formed. Marriage represents a central site of female power in *Viduvilt*. In this adaptation in particular, women are responsible for initiating massive conflicts, sometimes with extensive consequences, as well as the hero's central quest. Establishing a familial pedigree is, of course, dependent on marriage, the issue that catalyzes the story's main conflict. The final crisis of the Wigalois universe is usually the epic battle with count Lion of Namur, but in *Viduvilt*, that battle is replaced by a conflict between two maidens who both aim to marry Viduvilt, surrounded by their supporting cast of family members. One is the heiress of the formerly bewitched land that the Arthurian hero freed, and the other is a daughter of the family that Viduvilt reunites after fighting the dragon. Risking their own and their families' fates, each sets out to convince Viduvilt to become her groom; Lorel, daughter of the besieged kingdom's ruler, is the eventual victor. Of course, the hero's own backstory, as presented in all *Wigalois* adaptations, problematizes marriage, considering that the strange knight brings Gawein to his realm in order to preserve his lineage, a successful attempt in all adaptations as the birth of Wigalois/ Wigoleis/ Viduvilt illustrates. This time, women go out of their way to achieve the same result. *Viduvilt* introduces the motif of multiple brides to the Wigalois narrative,

---

**17** For further discussion of the dragon family, see Jaeger and Häberlein (Häberlein 2012, 76; Jaeger 2000, 271).

providing a platform for the exploration of women's agency through the politics of marriage.

In *Viduvilt*, marriage serves as the catalyst for the hero's primary narrative quest. Crucially, another seemingly minor change to the text underscores this development: the wild woman with whom Wigalois and Wigoleis had a harrowing (if humorous) encounter, has now become a mother – and not just any mother, but the mother of the knight's former archenemy, the "heathen" Roaz (here: nameless giant). In *Viduvilt*, the wild woman is a nameless figure, both courtly and un-courtly, living in a castle with an entourage of four hundred women like an Amazon. Although the narrator sometimes refers to her servants as demonic, he does abstain from deploying such terminology to describe the giant's mother – in contrast with other characters in the text, such as the king, who calls her "she-devil". *Viduvilt*'s description of the giant's mother does include residue of the comic irony found in *Wigalois*. However, the sexual connotations present in *Wigalois* and *Wigoleis* are completely eliminated from this text (as are all other scenes of sexual violence); the wild woman is not ridiculed either for her transgressions or for her attempts to seize agency.

This formerly comical figure, however, becomes a powerful person in *Viduvilt*, and is initially portrayed as responsible for all the sorrow befalling the characters. The text introduces the wild woman as a mother who is concerned for her bachelor son. As she sees it, Lorel the Fair, heiress of the formerly enchanted Korntin (now unnamed except for the reference to a mighty fortress with the name Waksenshteyn within its realm), would make the perfect bride-to-be. Unfortunately, the marital ambition of both the giant and his mother is met with opposition. Feeling scorned, the wild woman urges her son to besiege Lorel's family castle and kingdom, and she supports this endeavor with her magic. By this point, the mother's ambitious marriage plans have brought immense suffering on not only the royal family but also the whole country that she cursed and burned with sorcery. Subsequently, the queen sends the messenger maiden to secure support in the fight against the giant at King Arthur's court, promising her daughter as reward to the liberating knight in order to protect her kingdom. As the messenger maiden explains: "the lord who will take on the battle and defeat the same man and take the life of the mighty giant – my lady will give him her dearest daughter with her noble body as a lawful wife [...]." ([velkher iz der zelbig her der sikh des shtreytn vil nemn an [...] un dem shtarkn rizn nem zeyn lebn do vil im meyn fro ir libstn tokhter gebn mit irm shtolzn layp tsu aynem elikhen veyp.], *Viduvilt*, 20v).

The queen's husband is not completely absent from the unfolding events. Affected by the wild woman's enchantment, the king runs through the woods in the guise of a stag. When he jumps into a well and reemerges from it in his real form as a man, he promises his daughter's hand to Viduvilt in the event that the knight can successfully free his land from usurpation – which he believes to be unlikely, as he repeatedly emphasizes. Taking into account the queen's previous offer of her daughter's hand in marriage, the king's statement becomes a mere reiteration; the queen has already set the conditions for the liberation of country and castle. The unnecessary repetition of these conditions by the king merely reinforces the impression that men have lost agency in this text. Further evidence includes Viduvilt's comic name; the narrator's criticism of Gawein's behavior, the knight's inability to reunite his family, and the portrayal of a giant who acts according to his mother's wishes. The queen instead seizes agency, ruling over the fate of kin and kingdom. Not only is the text's central dispute the result of marriage politics; the events themselves focus more on the mothers than the princess or the giant. The children merely become tokens for their mothers' orchestrations.

## 4.3 Neither Lilith nor Eve: Revisiting Misogynist Role Models

If *triuwe* was the connecting feature among women in *Wigalois*, it has been replaced in *Viduvilt* by motherhood. Here, the wild woman fulfills several functions. She is now the mother of the Arthurian knight's former main opponent and triggers the story's initial conflict through her attempts to arrange her son's marriage. Furthermore, she helps the Arthurian knight intentionally and unintentionally by destroying an obstacle on his path and by sparing his life. And finally, *she* becomes Viduvilt's main opponent. This change affects the text's men significantly, as the former heathen Roaz is now a bachelor-giant with an overbearing mother. A maternal figure has replaced the wife of earlier editions. The resulting family dynamics and the question of how to fill the vacant partner position essentially drive the plot. In *Viduvilt*, mistaken revenge does not guide the wild woman's actions; instead, she is driven by good (albeit arguably consequential) intentions to protect and care for her son. Moreover, by intervening in her son's battles with Viduvilt, the knight becomes her enemy too, as she repeatedly announces. The protagonist threatens her son's life and even kills a number of her subordinates, provoking her immediate rage, which she expresses clearly: "Now tell me, you young villain, how can you consider me such a nothing that you dare to ride here so very boldly and wish to fight with my son and have additionally fought with my maidens? Most assuredly, I will not endure it from you!" ([Nu zog mir du yunger boys vikht vi halstu mikh azo gor for nihkt un doz du azo gor hofertig reydest un du wilst mit meynem zun her shtreytn un du host mir der tsu meyne meyd geslagn tsvar es vert dir nimer ver tragn], *Viduvilt*, 68v).

Despite her anger, however, the wild woman does not act upon her desire for revenge but shows clemency in a rather surprising twist. Rather than killing her son's opponent (also *her* opponent), the wild woman helps the hero, both deliberately and involuntarily. The fight between the wild woman and the knight is described across two encounters. During the first, more combative encounter, the wild woman hears Viduvilt's horse neigh and runs away, mistaking the sound for the scream of the dragon, a creature she thoroughly fears. While fleeing, she accidentally destroys the deadly mechanism of a bridge with moving wheels made of swords that blocked the castle's entrance (*Viduvilt*, 69v). In *Wigalois*, by contrast, God intervenes to destroy the mechanism following Wigalois' prayer for support (*Wigalois*, 6874–6899). Due to this seemingly minor plot change, the wild woman shifts from being a figure of mere comic relief to an important catalyst for the narrative's events. She not only sets the stage for the hero's primary quest but also inadvertently helps him, a move that was reserved for a divine power in the MHG adaptation.

The wild woman further helps the hero, intentionally this time, by saving his life. When Viduvilt enters the castle, a showdown with the giant's mother ensues, and she nearly kills him by spearing him in the armpit with a pole – which is supposed to remain in his armpit until his future wife pulls it out. The giant's mother grants Viduvilt his life on this one condition. In Witzenhausen's later adaptation, the wild woman's surprising mercy is explained by a few additional verses: a servant enters the scene, informing the giant's mother that Viduvilt killed the menacing dragon. Out of gratitude, she saves the Arthurian hero's life. This life-saving constraint again emphasizes that in *Viduvilt*, a woman determines the conditions to which the hero must agree. As he does with the queen of the besieged kingdom, Viduvilt takes an oath to uphold these conditions.

However, despite his seemingly honorable intentions, Viduvilt knowingly swears two oaths that are in direct conflict with one another. He can either spare the giant's life while breaking the promise to kill him (which he had offered to the queen of the besieged kingdom) or he can kill the giant and break his agreement with the giant's mother. Once he is out of the wild woman's direct range, Viduvilt choses the latter. On his way to Lorel's castle, Viduvilt meets and kills the giant. He grasps his sword in both hands, charges with force at the monstrous man and hews off one of his legs with a single stroke, so that he falls down like a sack. He then hews off his head. Even if Viduvilt is incapable of defeating the giant's mother, he kills the son and therefore gains victory. This victory seems fraudulent, however, and morally problematic, in light of the mother's mercy. The giant's mother herself worked within the courtly ethics system, demonstrating her capability for showing mercy and obligation when appropriate. Viduvilt, on the other hand, is faced with a choice between two obligations and decides in favor of a promising marriage and inheritance rather than saving the giant's life.

A fight with the giant's mother replaces the epic battle with the heathen Roaz, which is typically the central task for the Arthurian hero of the Wigalois universe. After *Viduvilt* kills the giant-usurper in passing, the wild woman becomes his new, morally ambiguous enemy, since her maternal nature justifies her anger and grief. Defined by her maternal status and replacing the ridiculed and grotesque Ruel of *Wigalois*, the wild woman becomes Viduvilt's dangerous yet merciful main adversary. This last fight scene reveals not Viduvilt's invincibility but rather his status as an ethically problematic individual. Rather than depicting the giant's mother as an overbearing parent drawing on standard misogynistic tropes, the text presents her deeds as positive and merciful in both encounters between her and Viduvilt. In contrast, Robert Warnock interprets the initial scene between the knight and the giant's mother, in which she shows him mercy, as an event that generates narrative suspense; their final fight, he argues, underscores the invincibility of the Arthurian knight (Warnock 1981, 101). In the case of the fight with the giant's mother, however, her invincibility is displayed. Viduvilt is not capable of defeating her independently but depends on her mercy to end the fight. The core combat scene from *Wigalois* now ends in a draw that is never solved.

The wild woman feels obliged to spare Viduvilt's life out of gratitude but imposes a condition, trusting Viduvilt's promise not to break the agreement. Although the bewitched king refers to the wild woman as a threat and she-devil, the narrator not only emphasizes her mercy but justifies her behavior in four ways, each connected to her maternal identity. First, she is a matriarch concerned about the continuation of her family line, and as such she is interested in finding a respectable match for her son. Second, as the text repeatedly assures the audience, from her perspective Viduvilt is a stranger, intruding on her marriage politics and threatening the life of her son – and in that fear, she is proven right. Third, she adheres to the knightly honor code by sparing Viduvilt's life out of gratitude, in contrast with the behavior of the Arthurian knight himself. And finally, she helps the hero by completing a task that belongs to God in a previous version of the narrative, destroying the mechanism of the sword bridge. All these changes seem minor in themselves but, in combination, paint the picture of a powerful female character guided by moral codes and the preservation of her lineage. The adaptor does not demonize her, but in fact empowers her throughout the text, giving her tasks that the hero and even God completed in *Wigalois* and *Wigoleis*.

Noting the Jewish background of the adaptor and audience, literature scholars Achim Jaeger and Neil Thomas have argued that the giant's mother is portrayed in a demonic light as homage to the most (in)famous mother in the Jewish-biblical tradition: Lilith, mother of demons and imminent threat to newborns, according to Kabbalistic belief (Jaeger 2000, 286; Thomas 2005, 61).[18] For Thomas, it is precisely the giant's mother's matriarchal qualities that make her appear demonic: "Something of the logic of matriarchal evil reappears in the Jewish versions, where the mother of 'Luzifer' is depicted as being an even more devilish figure than her son" (Thomas 2006, 61). This Luzifer reference from Thomas is an anachronism: Luzifer is not mentioned until Witzenhausen's seventeenth century adaptation, and this adaptation therefore does not support the argument that the giant's mother is depicted in a demonic light. Thomas' argument assumes that the male figure directly impacts the reception of the female figures – something common to the portrayal of female figures in *Wigalois* and *Wigoleis*. At the core of the *Viduvilt* adaptation, however, resides an abandonment of this depiction.

The emphasis on the wild-woman-as-demon, in order to argue for a Judaized adaptation, is further complicated by the fact that demons, in a Jewish tradition, are not simply evil and destructive, as Thomas and Jaeger have argued. Rather, as Astrid Lembke has shown, in Jewish literature, demons typically are represented as ambiguous and "human", obeying rules within human-demon relationships (Lembke 2013, 48, 39–40). The giant is neither portrayed as overtly evil nor does she bear enough Kabbalistic traces to mark her as a second Lilith. The case of the giant's mother is further complicated if we consider that *Wigalois* explicitly featured demons, such as those that removed the corpse of the heathen Roaz (*Wigalois*, 8136–8138). In contrast, the first known Yiddish adaptations refrain from introducing material with religious connotations and avoid depicting either the giant or his mother in a distinctly demonic light.

The giant's mother presents the most distinct and extensive revision of a character within the text, but she is only one example of the way in which the *Viduvilt* adaptor uses figures from *Wigalois* to push the boundaries of the patriarchal Arthurian world. The Old Yiddish *Viduvilt* not only increases the agency of

---

**18** Häberlein too follows Jaeger and Thomas in their argument that Lilith could function as a model for the giant's mother, although she admits this is only a possibility (Häberlein 2012, 82). The figure of Lilith as seductress and evil night-demon appears most prominently in the foundational text of Kabbalism, the Zohar (1:14b; 27b; 33b; 34b; 55a; 169b; 2:27b; 96a; 106a; 3:19a; 76b–77a).

women featured in other texts depicting the Wigalois universe. This adaptation also goes so far as to reverse gender roles completely. A seemingly minor change, often overlooked by scholars, occurs during a scene that takes place after Viduvilt's fight with the dragon. The unconscious knight is lying on the ground, at the mercy of a fisherman and his wife, who discover him. As in *Wigalois*, the fisherman and his wife plan to steal the knight's valuables and begin undressing him. Realizing that the knight is still alive, the fisherman decides to kill him and asks his wife to hand him a pick with which to murder Viduvilt. Gazing upon Viduvilt's features, she opposes her husband's plan: "O, how can it be in your heart that you wish to murder this young man? I have never seen his equal on earth." ([akh vi kanstu in deynem herzen hon dos du vilst der shlogen den yungen man zeyns gleykhens zakh ikh oyf erdn ni.], *Viduvilt*, 60r). The fisherman, however, is determined to go forward with his plan, abandoning it only after his wife blackmails him with sexual withdrawal. This is a complete inversion of the figures' roles in the narrative, in comparison to the Middle High German *Wigalois* — where, as Achim Jaeger remarks, the fisherman's wife is depicted as a second Eve. In that text, the wife suggests murder, introducing sin into the world and underscoring the text's misogyny (Jaeger 2000, 277). Alluding to divine providence, the fisherman can barely keep his wife from murdering Wigalois (*Wigalois*, 5387–5393). Moreover, the narrator of *Wigalois* connects this scene to a short misogynist excursion: "Even today a wicked woman is worse than any man, because she can never consider what will happen to her later." ("es ist ouch noch ein übel wîp wirser danne dehein man, wan sie niht bedenken kan waz ir dar nâch kümftic sî." *Wigalois*, 5394–5396). In *Viduvilt*, by contrast, the fisherman and his wife have completely changed their roles, and the woman saves the hero's life in defiance of her husband's plan to murder him. Like the wild woman, the fisherman's wife helps the protagonist, allowing him to continue with his quest. The women of *Viduvilt* not only possess agency, they use it to ensure the knight's success; they are even allowed to overrule men, as the fisherman's wife does with her husband. Moreover, the text includes neither any commentary critical of women's behavior nor any female characters as explicit comic relief, highlighting the fact that expressions of agency do not mark women as transgressive or morally suspect. In these ways, the adaptation empowers its female figures, from beginning to end.

## 4.4 Conclusion

Based on the examples discussed above, I have observed three main categories of change in the representation of women in *Viduvilt* as compared to the MHG

*Wigalois:* a positive re-evaluation of women, especially mothers; an increase in women's agency and consequent reduction in the title hero's own prowess; and an inversion of traditional gender roles. These changes become particularly visible in the portrayal of nuclear families in *Viduvilt*. At the heart of the family resides a strong matriarch, concerned with the preservation and continuation of the family line. Women figures are portrayed as *mater familias*, as mothers who lead their families; they reunite as well as expand their families, through marriage and childbirth. In *Viduvilt*, marriage emerges as a central field of conflict, but the conflict is largely dictated by women, with the Arthurian knight's central quest determined by women's conflicting interests.

Similar to historian Moshe Rosman's description of the role of Jewish women in early modern European society, women in *Viduvilt* function as facilitators of action, not just bystanders (Rosman 2008/2009, 414). Mothers in particular become leaders in the text. They make decisions that impact not only the hero's path but also the destiny of whole countries.[19] With its cast of influential women, *Viduvilt* presents a very different approach to the Arthurian source material than Wirnt's *Wigalois* but cannot be judged "deficient" or unfaithful. The *Viduvilt* adaptor draws on *Wigalois* as a model while making unorthodox representational choices. At first that seems contrary to the material and its background, but the adaptor does so without leaving the Arthurian narrative behind. Rather, some changes, such as the end without the epic "heathen" battles, underscore the adherence to the Middle High German Arthurian stories and the Early New High German adaptations. Further, as the earlier exploration of *Wigalois* has shown, the Middle High German text contains a conflicted representation of female figures, creating a narrative around a wide range of diverse female figures while ultimately restricting their agency. The *Wigoleis* adaptor chose to develop *Wigalois*' concept of devotion further while *Viduvilt* represents a text that maintains the inclusion of diverse women but grants them more power rather than restricting their identity. The *Viduvilt* adaptor does not lack awareness of an overarching framework; instead, he tries to solve the conflict inherent to the Wigalois tradition by borrowing the genre model of the Arthurian romance and basic structure of *Wigalois* and filling the narrative in a way meant to attract an early modern Yiddish-speaking audience.

Taking the classical angle of scholarship into account, the increase in women's agency and revision of female roles within a Yiddish text poses the question

---

**19** Elisheva Baumgarten has noted mothers' similar remarkable position in the 13th century Hebrew story collection *Sefer Hama'asim*, arguing that mothers play a much more active role in these stories than is typical of medieval Ashkenazi literature (Baumgarten 2017, 351–352).

of whether the adaptor views strong mothers and women from the Jewish Bible as literary models or archetypes – such as Deborah, who fights a war and leads the troops, or Esther, who prevents genocide. As counterparts to the patriarchs Abraham, Isaac, and Jacob, Judaism promotes the matriarchs Sarah, Rebecca, Rachel, and Leah, who also play an important role in liturgy. Taking into account the historical and cultural context in which the text emerged, one could see its representations as gesturing towards the slightly better situation of Jewish women in the medieval and early modern period. In contrast with their Christian counterparts, Jewish women could play active roles within marriage and the negotiation of economic matters, insofar as these matters pertained to the private family sphere, the Jewish woman's domain.[20]

Despite the fact that in medieval and early modern Jewish society "[w]omen had many roles, and motherhood was a central one," (Baumgarten 2004, 186) different, conflicting paradigms including strong misogynist beliefs about women's impurity existed in Jewish contemporaneous thought.[21] Jewish women in medieval and early modern Europe could often claim greater agency than those in surrounding Christian communities, but they still lived in a patriarchal society with all its consequential restrictions for women. Although these restrictions led to constant struggles (Grossman 2004, 2; Goldin 2011, 2), it is undeniable that the early modern Yiddish-speaking audience had an immense interest in fictional literature featuring strong Jewish women, as Astrid Lembke (2015, 79) has argued. Thus, the *Viduvilt* adaptor does not necessarily portray an accurate outer-literary historical situation but rather creates a functional utopia for maternal agency by, first, inverting gender roles within the text; second, promoting women – especially mothers – to starring roles, often while diminishing focus on men (even God); and, finally, by granting women authority over the hero and his fate. The issue of gender and agency turns this text into no less than an early modern Arthurian romance about women, a unique and unjustly overlooked part of this literary tradition.

---

**20** The significant role of women within the economic arena was a result of the crusades and the devastation they brought to Jewish communities, diminishing the number of men in society due to anti-Jewish violence. (Baskin 1998a, 19; Baskin 1998b, 102; Grossman 2004, 122; Goldin 2011, 236; Bell 2008, 121).

**21** Rashi, for example, perceived women as the pillar of the household, but warned against women straying from their homebound roles. Other prominent Jewish men, like Rabbi Asher ben Yechiel, were critical of the growing power of women, seeing it as a constant threat (Goldin 2011 62–63, 68, 74). See also Baskin 2013, 36, 48; Baumgarten 2012, 220.

# 5 Epilogue

As we have seen, in the Middle High German romance *Wigalois* (1210/1220) by Wirnt von Grafenberg, the audience encounters a bold statement: "A wise man is not governed by a woman's advice." ("Swer sînen rât læt an diu wîp, dern ist ein wîser man." *Wigalois*, 1358–1359). This remark serves two purposes. First, Wigalois, a soon-to-be Arthurian knight and son of Gawein, explains why, at this moment, he disregards his mother's concerns about embarking on a dangerous journey to the Arthurian court.[1] Wigalois' mother, the audience is told, is outright wrong – but not *just* his mother. In contrast, Viduvilt's mother's advice to her husband Gabein receives the narrator's endorsement: "And thereafter he [Gabein] came to regret that he did not wait for her counsel." ([un doz er ir rot nit beyt / doz wurd im dernokh leyd.], *Viduvilt*, 11r). Between these two extremes – a warning about the dangers of listening to women and a rebuke for not taking a woman's advice – the rich tradition of *Wigalois* adaptations unfolds and, along with it, the complex portrayal of women.

It is easy to dismiss *Wigalois* from a modern point of view as outdated and conservative. Yet, Wirnt's depiction of women is complex and conflicted, and later adaptations address this fact, each in their own way. All three texts explored in this book grapple with the issue of gender and women's agency in some form. Wirnt's thirteenth-century text presents a wide array of female roles but simultaneously restricts "correct" female behavior to courtly devotion and passivity. At the core of the text, women depend on a male counterpart, especially in the common trope of the damsel-in-distress, which is deployed multiple times throughout *Wigalois*. Nevertheless, we have also seen that *Wigalois* exceeds the mere portrayal of women as passive through the emphasis on the border-crossing power the adaptor attributes to the women's constancy and devotion (*triuwe*). In other words, through their focus on an object of devotion, women are unified, a feature enabling the deconstruction of cultural-religious borders between the narrative's Christian and "heathen" characters. The concept of *triuwe* allows women to briefly exceed their otherwise restricted roles, though it still ultimately results in a woman's death in response to the loss of her male counterpart.

The early modern *Wigoleis* transforms the concept of devotion into admiration with the mere presence of women rendering a knight's deeds heroic. Death remains a unifying force for women in *Wigoleis* but loses its potential as an em-

---

[1] This quote is sometimes mistakenly attributed to the narrator, although preceded and followed by Wigalois' speech.

powering experience through the loss of its association with the concept of *triuwe*, the central means through which women express agency in *Wigalois*. Out of all women, one has a significant role in the text: Mary, mother of Jesus. Mary, however, appears not as a figure within the text, but as a heavenly model for characters' behavior, informing the depiction of several important characters and aiding both the narrator and the hero in their respective projects. In *Wigoleis*, fidelity to Mary overpowers even a concern for one's own death. This representational strategy pays off, as this adaptation proves incredibly popular over the following 100 years of the developing Catholic-Protestant schism, for both Catholic and Protestant audiences. Women in the text who resemble Mary are admired and honored by the narrator and serve as role models for a male as well as a female audience due to Mary's unflinching devotion to Christ.

Exploring the potential for female agency that is also a part of *Wigalois'* women, the *Viduvilt* adaptor revises the text's portrayal of both the women and female otherworldly creatures of the Wigalois universe, turning them all into mothers, from the damsel-in-distress to the dragon. In *Viduvilt*, the maternal theme is so broadly expanded that mothers, due to concerns over their children's marriage prospects, are now responsible for the besiegement of an entire country. These maternal narrative revisions lead to an increase in the number of active women and other female characters; women play an indispensable role in the negotiation of dynastic lines. Significantly, the Yiddish adaptation omits sexual violence entirely, eliminating one especially problematic representation of gender relations typically found in Wigalois stories.

Later German and Yiddish adaptations of Wigalois stories do not carry forward the dominant discourse on women's agency evident in *Wigalois* and *Wigoleis:* one text unifies women through *triuwe* while the other presents mother Mary as a pious role model rather than driver of the narrative. *Viduvilt*'s maternal theme is also not retained in later retellings. Rather, most newer narratives' increasing focus on one knight and his combat adventures prevails. In the direct *Viduvilt* successor, *Ritter Gabein* [Sir Gabein] (Frankfurt an der Oder, 1789), Viduvilt's mother remains alive at the end of the story.

In the most recent adaptation, the graphic novel *Die phantastischen Abenteuer des Glücksritters Wigalois* [The Fantastic Adventures of Wigalois, Knight of Fortune] (2004), a new woman is introduced, occupying the position of Wirnt von Grafenberg's muse. She encourages the author to share the knight's story with his audience – and, ultimately, with us. The addition of a muse emphasizes the medieval trope of women as patrons, inspiring the writing of vernacular knightly romances and therewith justifying their composition in the first place. The modern adaptation further mirrors Ferdinand Roth's parodistic *Vom Könige Artus und von dem bildschönen Ritter Wieduwilt. Ein Ammenmährchen* [About

King Arthur and the beautiful Sir Wieduwilt. An Old Wives' Tale] (1786) which opens with a dedication to the narrator's fictional former nurse, depicted as an old spinster. These texts' emphasis on women is nonetheless brief, and never returns women to the extraordinary position they held in the shared adaptation tradition's past. None of these adaptations draws from the radical way women are integrated in the first Yiddish adaptation. *Viduvilt* remains an exception. However, as my analysis of *Wigalois* and *Wigoleis* has shown, these texts' grappling with the gendered aspects of characters' agency heavily impacts the portrayal of *all* characters as well as the direction of the unfolding narratives. In future scholarship, revisiting the vast number of *Wigalois* adaptations through the lens of the construction of female roles will help bring these adaptations into critical dialogue with their literary predecessors and likely reveal much about contemporaneous gender modes through audiences' continued fascination with the human need to tell stories. Albeit pre-modern, all three texts discussed here present women in more empowering roles than in either of the two most recent Arthurian Hollywood movie adaptations. Or, in other words, contemporary adaptations of medieval material are closer to what mass culture classifies as "medieval".

# Bibliography

Ader, Dorothee. *Prosaversionen höfischer Epen in Text und Bild. Zur Rezeption des 'Tristrant' im 15. und 16. Jahrhundert.* Heidelberg: Universitätsverlag Winter, 2010.
Bachorski, Hans-Jürgen, and Helga Sciurie. "Einleitung." *Eros – Macht – Askese. Geschlechterspannungen als Dialogstruktur in Kunst und Literatur.* Eds. Helga Sciurie and Hans-Jürgen Bachorski. Trier: Wissenschaftlicher Verlag Trier, 1996. 9–22.
Bartoll, Jordi, Isidre Monés, and Manfred Schwab. *Die phantastischen Abenteuer des Glücksritters Wigalois.* Forchheim: Kulturamt des Landkreises Forchheim, 2011.
Baskin, Judith R. "Introduction." *Jewish Women in Historical Perspective.* Ed. Judith R. Baskin. Detroit: Wayne State University Press, 1998a. 15–24.
Baskin, Judith R. "Jewish Women in the Middle Ages." *Jewish Women in Historical Perspective.* Ed. Judith R. Baskin. Detroit: Wayne State University Press, 1998b. 101–127.
Baskin, Judith R. "Jewish Traditions about Women and Gender Roles." *Women and Gender in Medieval Europe.* Eds. Judith Bennett and Ruth Mazo Karras. Oxford: Oxford University Press, 2013. 36–51.
Baumgarten, Elisheva. *Mothers and Children: Jewish Family Life in Medieval Europe.* Princeton: Princeton University Press, 2004.
Baumgarten, Elisheva. "Mothers and Ma'asim: Maternal Roles in Medieval Hebrew Tales." *Mothers in the Jewish Cultural Imagination.* Eds. Marjorie Suzan Lehman, Jane L. Kanarek and Simon J. Bronner. Oxford; Portland: The Littman Library of Jewish Civilization, 2017. 345–357.
Baumgarten, Elisheva. "Gender and Daily Life in Jewish Communities." *The Oxford Handbook of Women and Gender in Medieval Europe.* Eds. Judith Bennett and Ruth Karras. Oxford: Oxford University Press, 2012. 213–228.
Baumgarten, Jean. *Introduction to Old Yiddish Literature.* Translated by Jerold Frakes, Oxford University Press, 2005.
Beifuss, Helmut. *Wigalois – Ein Ritter Gottes: Eine Handlungsanalytische Studie.* Hamburg. Verlag Dr. Kovač, 2016.
Bell, Dean Phillip. *Jews in the Early Modern World.* Lanham: Rowman & Littlefield, 2008.
Bendheim, Amelie. *Wechselrahmen: Medienhistorische Fallstudien zum Romananfang des 13. Jahrhunderts.* Heidelberg: Universitätsverlag Winter, 2017.
Bennewitz, Ingrid. "Darumb lieben Toechter / seyt nicht zu gar fürwitzig…. Deutschsprachige moralisch-didaktische Literatur des 13.–15. Jahrhunderts." *Geschichte der Mädchen- und Frauenbildung.* Eds. Elke Kleinau and Claudia Opitz. Frankfurt am Main; New York: Campus Verlag, 1996. 23–41.
Berger, Shlomo. "Functioning Within a Diasporic Third Space: The Case of Early Modern Yiddish." *Jewish Studies Quarterly* 15.1 (2008): 68–86.
Bertelsmeier-Kierst, Christa. "Die Krakauer 'Wigalois' Fragmente (q). Eine weitere Handschrift im Umkreis der Cgm 19-Gruppe?" *Zeitschrift für deutsches Altertum und deutsche Literatur* 144 (2015): 150–177.
Böcking, Cordula. "'daz wær ouch noch guot wîbes sit.' Streitbare Frauen in Wirnts *Wigalois*." *Aktuelle Tendenzen der Artusforschung.* Eds. Brigitte Burrichter et al. Berlin; Boston: De Gruyter, 2013. 363–380.
Böhme, Hartmut. "Vorwort." *Übersetzung und Transformation. 1. Jahrestagung des SFB Transformationen der Antike.* Eds. Hartmut Böhme et al. Berlin: De Gruyter, 2007. v–xiii.

Boyer, Tina. *The Giant Hero in Medieval Literature*. Leiden; Boston: Brill, 2016.
Brandstetter, Alois. *Prosaauflösung: Studien Zur Rezeption der Höfischen Epik im Frühneuhochdeutschen Prosaroman*. Frankfurt am Main: Athenäum, 1971.
Brinker-von der Heyde, Claudia. *Geliebte Mütter, mütterliche Geliebte. Rolleninszenierung in höfischen Romanen*. Bonn: Bouvier, 1996.
Brinker-von der Heyde, Claudia. "'Hie ist diu aventiure geholt!' Die Jenseitsreise im *Wigalois* des Wirnt von Grafenberg: Kreuzzugspropaganda und unterhaltsame Glaubenslehre?" *Contemplata aliis tradere. Studien zum Verhältnis von Literatur und Spiritualität* (1995): 87–110.
Brown, James Hamilton. "Poetry as Source for Illustrated Prose: The 1519 Strassburg 'Wigoleis vom Rade'." *Fifteenth Century Studies* 34 (2009): 24–47.
Brown, James Hamilton. *Imagining the Text. Ekphrasis and Envisioning Courtly Identity in Wirnt von Gravenberg's 'Wigalois'*. Leiden: Brill, 2016.
Bruhn, Jørgen. "Dialogizing Adaptation Studies: From One-Way Transport to a Dialogic Two-Way Process." *Adaptation Studies: New Challenges, New Directions*. Eds. Jørgen Bruhn et al. New York: Bloomsbury Academic, 2013. 69–88.
Burns, E. Jane. "Performing Courtliness". *The Oxford Handbook of Women and Gender in Medieval Europe*. Eds. Judith M. Bennett and Ruth Mazo Karras. Oxford: Oxford University Press, 2013. 396–414.
Busch, Nathanael. "'bî den selben zîten / was daz gewonlîch.' Stellen allein reisende Frauen ein Problem dar?" *Artusroman und Mythos*. Eds. Friedrich Wolfzettel et al. Berlin; Boston: De Gruyter, 2011. 127–144.
Cahill, Ann J. *Rethinking Rape*. Ithaca: Cornell University Press, 2001.
Chrétien de Troyes. *Yvain: The Knight of The Lion*. Translated by Burton Raffel, Yale University Press, 1987.
Classen, Albrecht. "Gewaltverbrechen als Thema des spätarturischen Romans. Sozialkritisches in Wirnts von Grafenberg *Wigalois*." *Etudes germaniques* 62.2 (2007): 429–456.
Classen, Albrecht. "Schweigen und Reden in Hartmanns von Aue *Erec*." *Erec, ou, L'ouverture du monde arthurien: actes du colloque du Centre d'études médiévales de l'Université de Picardie-Jules Verne, Amiens, 16–17 janvier 1993*. Eds. Danielle Buschinger et al. Greifswald: Reineke Verlag, 1993. 25–42.
Classen, Albrecht. *Sexual Violence and Rape in the Middle Ages: A Critical Discourse in Premodern German and European Literature*. Berlin; Boston: De Gruyter, 2011.
Classen, Albrecht. *The German Volksbuch: A Critical History of a Late-Medieval Genre*. Lewiston: Edwin Mellen Press, 1995.
Clover, Carol J.: "Maiden Warriors and Other Sons." *The Journal of English and Germanic Philology* 85.1 (1986): 35–49.
Cormeau, Christoph. "Die jiddische Tradition von Wirnts *Wigalois*: Bemerkungen zum Fortleben einer Fabel unter veränderten Bedingungen." *LiLi Zeitschrift für Literaturwissenschaft und Linguistik* 8.22 (1978): 28–44.
Dallapiazza, Michael, "Spätmittelalterliche Ehedidaktik." *Liebe – Ehe – Ehebruch in der Literatur des Mittelalters*. Eds. Xenia von Ertzdorff-Kupfer and Marianne Wynn. Gießen: W. Schmitz, 1983. 161–172.

Däumer, Matthias, "Das Lachen des verbitterten Idealisten. Parodie und Satire im *Widuwilt*." *Ironie, Polemik und Provokation*. Eds. Cora Dietl, Christoph Schanze, and Friedrich Wolfzettel. Berlin; Boston: De Gruyter, 2014. 259–285.

Dietl, Cora. "Wigalois der Schachkönig." *Text und Kontext* 24 (2002): 98–112.

Dreeßen, Wulf-Otto. "Wigalois – Widuwilt. Wandlungen des Artusromans im Jiddischen." *Westjiddisch. Mündlichkeit und Schriftlichkeit/ Le Yiddish occidental. Actes du colloque de Mulhouse* 1 (1994): 84–98.

*Ein gar schöne liepliche und kurtzweilige History Von dem Edelen herren Wigoleis vom Rade. Ein Ritter von der Tafelronde. Mit seinen schönen hystorien und figuren/ Wie er geborn/ vnnd sein leben von seiner jugent an Biß an sein ende gefürt vnnd vollbracht hat*. Ed. Johann Knoblauch, 2nd ed., Straßburg, 1519.

Elukin, Jonathan. *Living Together, Living Apart: Rethinking Jewish-Christian Relations in the Middle Ages*. Princeton: Princeton University Press, 2013.

Elye Bokher. *Bovo d'Antona. A Yiddish Romance*. Critical edition with commentary by Claudia Rosenzweig. Leiden: Brill, 2016

Eming, Jutta. *Funktionswandel des Wunderbaren: Studien zum Bel Inconnu, zum Wigalois und zum Wigoleys vom Rade*. Trier: Wissenschaftlicher Verlag Trier, 1999.

Erasmus von Rotterdam. *Lob der Narrheit*. Edited and translated by Wilhelm Gottlieb Becker, Basel, 1780.

Fasbender, Christoph. "Gwigalois' Bergung: Zur Epiphanie des Helden als Erlöser." *Aktuelle Tendenzen der Artusforschung*. Ed. Brigitte Burrichter et al. Berlin; Boston: De Gruyter, 2013. 209–222.

Fasbender, Christoph. *Der 'Wigalois' Wirnts von Grafenberg: Eine Einführung*. Berlin: De Gruyter, 2010.

Fenster, Thelma S. "Introduction." *Arthurian Women: A Casebook*. Ed. Thelma S. Fenster. New York: Routledge, 1996. xvii–lxv.

Flood, John L. "Die schwere Geburt des Herrn Wigoleys vom Rade. Zur Entstehung und Formfindung eines frühneuzeitlichen Prosaromans." *Scrinium Berolinense: Tilo Brandis zum 65. Geburtstag*. Eds. Peter Jörg Becker et al. Wiesbaden: Reichert, 2000. 768–778.

Frakes, Jerold. *Early Yiddish Epic*. New York: Syracuse University Press, 2014.

Frakes, Jerold. *The Politics of Interpretation: Alterity and Ideology in Old Yiddish Studies*. Albany: State University of New York Press, 1988.

Frakes, Jerold. *Vernacular and Latin Literary Discourses of the Muslim Other in Medieval Germany*. New York: Palgrave Macmillan, 2011.

Fries, Maureen. "Female Heroes, Heroines, and Counter-Heroes: Images of Women in Arthurian Tradition." *Arthurian Women: A Casebook*. Ed. Thelma S. Fenster. New York: Routledge, 1996. 59–76.

Fuchs, Stephan. *Hybride Helden: Gwigalois und Willehalm. Beiträge zum Heldenbild und zur Poetik des Romans im frühen 13. Jahrhundert*. Heidelberg: Universitätsverlag Winter, 1997.

Goldin, Simha. *Jewish Women in Europe in the Middle Ages*. Manchester: Manchester University Press, 2011.

Grafetstätter, Andrea. "'Nur was du nie gesehen wird ewig dauern:' weiblich besetzte Bildprogramme im *Wigalois*." *Aktuelle Tendenzen der Artusforschung*. Ed. Brigitte Burrichter. Berlin; Boston: De Gruyter, 2013. 381–302.

Gravdal, Kathryn. *Ravishing Maidens: Writing Rape in Medieval French Literature and Law.* Philadelphia: University of Pennsylvania Press, 1991.
Grossman, Avraham. *Pious and Rebellious: Jewish Women in Medieval Europe.* Waltham: Brandeis University Press, 2004.
Grubmüller, Klaus. "Artusroman und Heilsbringerethos: Zum *Wigalois* des Wirnt von Gravenberg." *Beiträge zur Geschichte der deutschen Sprache und Literatur* 107 (1985): 218–239.
Häberlein, Bianca. "Transformationen religiöser und profaner Motive in *Wigalois, Widuwilt* und *Ammenmaehrchen*." *Rezeptionskulturen: Fünfhundert Jahre literarischer Mittelalterrezeption zwischen Kanon und Populärkultur.* Eds. Mathias Herweg and Stefan Keppler-Tasaki. Berlin; Boston: De Gruyter, 2012. 66–86.
Hahn, Ingrid. "Gott und Minne, Tod und triuwe: Zur Konzeption des *Wigalois* des Wirnt von Grafenberg." *Personenbeziehungen in der mittelalterlichen Literatur.* Eds. Helmut Brall, Barbara Haupt, and Urban Küsters. Düsseldorf: Droste, 1994. 37–60.
Heal, Bridget. *The Cult of Virgin Mary in Early Modern Germany: Protestant and Catholic Piety, 1500–1648.* Cambridge: Cambridge University Press, 2007.
Heine, Heinrich. *Gesammelte Werke. Kritische Gesammtausgabe.* Ed. Gustav Karpeles, vol. 5, G. Grothe'sche Verlagsbuchhandlung, 1887.
Heinzle, Joachim. "Über den Aufbau des *Wigalois*." *Euphorion. Zeitschrift für Literaturgeschichte* 67 (1973): 261–271.
Henderson, Ingeborg. "Dark Figures and Eschatological Images in Wirnt von Gravenberg's *Wigalois*." In *The Dark Figure in Medieval German and Germanic Literature.* Eds. Edward R. Haymes and Stephanie Cain Van d'Elden. Göppingen: Kümmerle, 1986. 99–113.
Henry, April. *The Female Lament: Agency and Gender in Medieval German Literature.* 2008. University of North Carolina at Chapel Hill, PhD dissertation.
Howard, John Anderson. *Hebrew-German and Early Yiddish Literature: A Survey of Problems.* 1972. University of Illinois at Urbana-Champaign, PhD dissertation.
Hutcheon, Linda. *A Theory of Adaptation.* London: Routledge, 2006.
Jaeger, Achim. *Ein jüdischer Artusritter.* Leipzig: S. Hirzel, 2000.
Kasper, Christine. *Von miesen Rittern und sündhaften Frauen und solchen die besser waren. Tugend- und Keuschheitsproben in der mittelalterlichen Literatur vornehmlich des deutschen Sprachraums.* Göttingen: Kümmerle, 1995.
Kasper-Marienberg, Verena. "Gemeinsamer Alltag–Geteilter Lebensraum? Der Frankfurter Wochenmarkt Als Christlich-Jüdischer Begegnungsort." *Aschkenas. Zeitschrift für Geschichte und Kultur der Juden* 26.2 (2016): 327–349.
Katz, Dovid. *Yiddish and Power.* Basingstoke; Hampshire: Palgrave Macmillan, 2015.
Kelly-Gadol, Joan. "Did Women have a Renaissance?" *Becoming Visible. Women in European History.* Eds. Renate Bridenthal and Claudia Koonz. Boston: Houghton Mifflin, 1977. 174–201.
*King Arthur.* Dir. Antoine Fuqua. Touchstone Home Entertainment, 2004.
*King Arthur: Legend of the Sword.* Dir. Guy Ritchie. Warner Bros., 2017.
Klein, Dorothea. "Geschlecht und Gewalt. Zur Konstitution von Männlichkeit im *Erec* Hartmanns von Aue." *Literarische Leben.* Eds. Matthias Meyer et al. Tübingen: Niemeyer, 2002. 433–463.
Knaeble, Susanne. "Ironische Distanzierung im Fokus intertextuellen Erzählens. Der westjiddische *Widuwilt* als Rezeptionsgegenstand." *Ironie, Polemik und Provokation.*

Eds. Cora Dietl, Christoph Schanze, and Friedrich Wolfzettel. Berlin; Boston: De Gruyter, 2014. 85–108.

Kristeller, Paul. *Die Strassburger Bücher-Illustration im 15. und im Anfange des 16. Jahrhunderts.* Leipzig: Seemann, 1888.

Krueger, Roberta. "Desire, Meaning, and the Female Reader: The Problem in Chrétien's *Charrete.*" *Lancelot and Guinevere: A Casebook.* Ed. Lori J. Walters. New York: Garland, 1996. 229–245.

*Kudrun.* Edited and Translated by Uta Störmer-Caysa. Stuttgart: Reclam, 2010.

Laube, Daniela. "The Stylistic Development of German Book Illustrations, 1460–1511." *A Heavenly Craft. The Woodcut in Early Printed Books.* Ed. Daniel de Simone. New York: George Braziller, 2004. 47–71.

Leidinger, Simone. "Überlegungen zur Minnehandlung und zur Treue in Wirnts Wigalois." *Aktuelle Tendenzen der Artusforschung.* Eds. Brigitte Burrichter et al. Berlin; Boston: De Gruyter, 2013. 403–420.

Leitch, Thomas. "Adaptation, the Genre." *Adaptation* 2 (2008): 106–210.

Lembke, Astrid. *Dämonische Allianzen, Jüdische Martenehenerzählungen der Europäischen Vormoderne.* Tübingen: A. Francke Verlag, 2013.

Lembke, Astrid. "Die Toten im Dritten Raum: Grabmäler als Orte der Begegnung zwischen Angehörigen verschiedener Religionen bei Wolfram von Eschenbach und Wirnt von Grafenberg." *Seminar* 53.1 (2017): 21–42.

Lembke, Astrid. "Ritter außer Gefecht. Konzepte passiver Bewährung im *Wigalois* und im *Widuwilt*." *Aschkenas* 25 (2015): 63–82.

Leviant, Kurt. *King Artus. A Hebrew Arthurian Romance of 1279 (MS. Cod. Vat. Hebr. Urbino 48, ff. 75–77.* New York: Ktav, 1969.

Lichtblau, Karin. "ein tier sô wol getân: Zum Motiv der Tierverwandlung im *Wigalois* des Wirnt von Grafenberg." *Tierverwandlungen. Codierungen und Diskurse.* Eds. Willem de Blécourt and Christa Agnes Tuczay. Tübingen: Francke Verlag, 2011. 221–239.

Linn, Irving. *Widwilt, Son of Gawain.* 1946. New York University, PhD Dissertation.

Lohbeck, Gisela. *Wigalois: Struktur der 'bezeichenunge.'* Frankfurt am Main: Peter Lang, 1991.

McLaughlin, Megan. "The Woman Warrior. Gender, Warfare and Society in Medieval Europe." *Women's Studies* 17 (1990): 193–209.

Melzer, Helmut. *Trivialisierungstendenzen im Volksbuch. Ein Vergleich der Volksbücher Tristrant und Isalde, Wigoleis und Wilhelm von Österreich mit den mittelhochdeutschen Epen.* Hildesheim: G. Olms, 1972.

Mertens, Volker. "Iwein und Gwigalois – der Weg zur Landesherrschaft." *Germanisch-romanische Monatsschrift* 31 NF (1981): 14–31.

Müller, Jan-Dirk. "Volksbuch/Prosaroman im 15./16. Jahrhundert. Perspektiven der Forschung." *Internationales Archiv für Sozialgeschichte der deutschen Literatur* 1. Sonderheft (1985): 1–128.

Müller, Maria E. *Jungfräulichkeit in Versepen des 12. und 13. Jahrhunderts.* München: Fink, 1995.

*OED Online*, Oxford University Press, www.oed.com/view/Entry/3851 (22 October 2018).

Oergel, Maike. *The Return of King Arthur and the Nibelungen: National Myth in Nineteenth Century English and German Literature.* Berlin: De Gruyter, 1998.

Przybilski, Martin. "Ein anti-arthurischer Artusroman. Invektiven gegen die höfische Literatur zwischen den Zeilen des 'Melech Artus'." *Zeitschrift für deutsches Altertum und deutsche Literatur* 131 (2002): 409–435.

Quinlan, Jessica. "One of Us Is Lying: The Narrator, Gauvain and the Pucelle de Lis." *Aktuelle Tendenzen der Artusforschung*. Eds. Brigitte Burrichter et al. Berlin; Boston: De Gruyter, 2013. 39–53.

Rasmussen, Ann Marie. "The Women in Gottfried's *Tristan and Isolde*." *A Companion to Gottfried von Strassburg's Tristan*. Ed. Will Hasty. Woodbridge; Suffolk: Boydell & Brewer. 137–158.

"Ritterliche History des Hochberühmpten und Thewren Ritters Herrn Wigoleis vom Rade…" *Buch der Liebe*. Ed. Sigmund Feyerabend. Frankfurt, 1587. 382–396.

Rosman, Moshe. "The Early Modern European 'Jewish Woman'." *Journal of Ukrainian Studies* 33–34 (2008–2009): 407–416.

[Roth, Ferdinand]. *Vom König Artus und von dem bildschönen Ritter Wieduwilt. Ein Ammenmährchen*. Leipzig: Verlag der Dykischen Buchhandlung, 1786.

Rovang, Paul R. "Hebraizing Arthurian Romance: The Originality of Melech Artus." *Arthuriana* 19 (2009): 3–9.

Rubin, Miri. *Mother of God: A History of the Virgin Mary*. New Haven: Yale University Press, 2009.

Schnyder, André. "Der deutsche Prosaroman des 15. und 16. Jahrhunderts. Ein Problemfeld, eine Tagung und der Versuch einer Bilanz." *Eulenspiegel trifft Melusine. Der frühneuhochdeutsche Prosaroman im Licht neuer Forschungen und Methoden*. Eds. Catherine Drittenbass et al. Amsterdam: Rodopi, 2010. 11–39.

Schönhoff, Judith. *Von 'werden degen' und 'edelen vrouwen' zu 'tugentlichen helden' und 'eelichen hausfrawen'. Zum Wandel der Konzepte von Weiblichkeit und Männlichkeit in den Prosaauflösungen Mittelhochdeutscher Epen*. Frankfurt am Main: Peter Lang, 2008.

Schröder, Werner. "Der synkretistische Roman des Wirnt von Gravenberg." *Euphorion* 80 (1986): 235–277.

Schwind, Klaus. "Komisch." *Ästhetische Grundbegriffe*, vol. 3, eds. Karlheinz Barck et al. Stuttgart: Metzler, 2001. 32–384.

Selmayr, Pia. *Der Lauf der Dinge. Wechselverhältnisse zwischen Raum, Ding und Figur bei der narrativen Konstitution von Anderwelten im 'Wigalois' und im 'Lanzelet'*. Frankfurt am Main: Peter Lang, 2017.

Söll, Georg. "Maria in der Geschichte von Theologie und Frömmigkeit." *Handbuch der Marienkunde*. Eds. Wolfgang Beinert and Heinrich Petri. Regensburg: Pustet, 1984. 93–231.

Sperling, Jutta Gisela. *Medieval and Renaissance Lactations: Images, Rhetorics, Practices*. Farnham; Burlington: Ashgate, 2013.

Stange, Carmen. "Florie und die anderen. Frauenfiguren im *Wigalois* Wirnts von Grafenberg." *Mertens lesen. Exemplarische Lektüren für Volker Mertens zum 75. Geburtstag*. Eds. Carmen Stange et al. Göttingen: V&R Unipress, 2012. 127–146.

Sterling-Hellenbrand, Alexandra. *Topographies of Gender in Middle High German Arthurian Romances*. New York: Garland Publishing, 2001.

Tarantul, Evgen. "Wie fanden die Riesen ihren Weg in die Altjiddische Literatur und woher kommen Sie?" *Arcadia* 37.2 (2002): 384–395.

Thomas, Neil. "Wigalois and Parzival. Father and Son Roles in the German Romance of Gawain's Son." *Arthurian Studies in Honor of P. J. C. Field*. Ed. Bonnie Wheeler. Cambridge: D.S. Brewer, 2004. 101–116.
Thomas, Neil. "Wirnt von Gravenberg's *Wigalois* and Heinrich von dem Türlin's *Diu Crône*." *German Literature of the High Middle Ages*. Ed. Will Hasty. New York: Camden, 2006. 203–214.
Thomas, Neil. *A German View of Camelot: Wirnt von Gravenberg's Wigalois and Arthurian Tradition*. Bern: Peter Lang, 1987.
Thomas, Neil. *Wirnt of Gravenberg's Wigalois: Intertextuality and Interpretation*. Cambridge: D. S. Brewer, 2005.
Timm, Erika. "Wie Elia Levita sein Bovobuch für den Druck überarbeitete. Ein Kapitel aus der italo-jiddischen Literatur der Renaissancezeit." *Germanisch-Romanische Monatsschrift* 72 (1991): 61–81.
Uhland, Ludwig. "Ritter Wieduwilt." *Gedichte. Vollständige kritische Ausgabe auf Grund des handschriftlichen Nachlasses*, vol. 2, eds. Erich Schmidt and Julius Hartmann. Stuttgart: J. G. Cotta Nachf., 1898. 159–161.
Ulrich von Zatzikhoven. *Lanzelet*. Edited and translated by Florian Kragl. Berlin; Boston: De Gruyter, 2013.
Valles, Margot B. *Judaized Romance and Romanticized Judaization: Adaptation in Hebrew and Early Yiddish Chivalric Literature*. 2013. Indiana University, PhD dissertation.
van D'Elden, Cain. "Specific and Generic Scenes in Verse *Tristan* Illustrations." *Visuality and Materiality in the Story of Tristan and Isolde*. Eds. Jutta Eming, Ann Marie Rasmussen, and Kathryn Starkey. Notre Dame: University of Notre Dame Press, 2012. 269–298.
Velten, Hans Rudolf. "Text und Lachgemeinschaft. Zur Funktion des Gruppenlachens bei Hofe in der Schwankliteratur." *Lachgemeinschaften. Kulturelle Inszenierungen und soziale Wirkungen von Gelächter im Mittelalter und in der Frühen Neuzeit*. Eds. Werner Röcke and Hans Rudolf Velten. Berlin: De Gruyter, 2005. 125–144.
*Viduvilt*. Cambridge, Wren Library. MS F.12.44 [16th ct.].
*Viduvilt*. Hamburg, Staats- und Universitätsbibliothek, Cod. Hebr. 255 [16th ct.].
*Viduvilt*. Hamburg, Staats- und Universitätsbibliothek, Cod. Hebr. 289 [16th ct.].
Wagenseil, Johann Christoph. *Belehrung der jüdisch-teutschen Red- und Schreibart* ... Königsberg, 1699.
Wandhoff, Heiko. "Gefährliche Blicke und rettende Stimmen. Eine audiovisuelle Choreographie von Minne und Ehe in Hartmanns *Erec*." *"Aufführung" und "Schrift" in Mittelalter und früher Neuzeit*. Ed. Jan-Dirk Müller. Stuttgart: Metzler 1996. 170–189.
Warnock, Robert G. "Wirkungsabsicht und Bearbeitungstechnik im Altjiddischen 'Artushof.'" *Zeitschrift für deutsche Philologie* 100 Sonderheft (1981): 98–109.
Weidenmüller, Otto. *Das Volksbuch von Wigoleis vom Rade*. 1910. Universität Göttingen, PhD dissertation.
Wennerhold, Markus. *Späte Mittelhochdeutsche Artusromane: "Lanzelet", "Wigalois", "Daniel von dem blühenden Tal", "diu Crône". Bilanz der Forschung 1960–2000*. Würzburg: Königshausen & Neumann, 2005.
Wenzel, Horst. "Herzeloyde und Sigune – Mutter und Geliebte. Zur Ikonographie der Liebe im Überschneidungsfeld von Text und Bild." *Eros – Macht – Askese. Geschlechterspannungen als Dialogstruktur in Kunst und Literatur*. Eds. Helga Sciurie and Hans-Jürgen Bachorski. Trier: Wissenschaftlicher Verlag Trier, 1996. 211–234.

Wenzel, Horst. *Hören und Sehen, Schrift und Bild. Kultur und Gedächtnis im Mittelalter.* München: C.H. Beck, 1995.
Wexler, Paul. *Three Heirs to a Judeo-Latin Legacy: Judeo-Ibero-Romance, Yiddish and Rotwelsch.* Wiesbaden: Harrassowitz, 1988.
"Wieduwilt." *Erzehlungen aus dem Heldenalter teutscher Nationen.* Ed. Daniel Ernst Wagner. Danzig, 1780. 382–517.
Wiesner, Merry E. *Gender, Church, and State in Early Modern Germany.* London: Longman, 1998.
"Wigoleis." *Buch der Abenteuer der Ritter von der Tafelrunde.* Ed. Ulrich Füetrer (1496–1500), 75 r.–83r. CGM 1, Bayerische Staatsbibliothek.
Wild, Inga. *Zur Überlieferung und Rezeption des "Kudrun"-Epos.* Göppingen: Kümmerle, 1979.
Wirnt von Grafenberg. *Wigalois.* Leiden: Universiteitsbibliotheek Leiden, LTK 537 [ca. 1372].
Wirnt von Grafenberg. *Wigalois. Der Ritter mit dem Rade. Erster Band:* Text. Ed. J.M.N. Kapteyn. Bonn: Klopp, 1926.
Wirnt von Grafenberg. *Wigalois. The Knight of Fortune's Wheel.* Translated and with an introduction by J. W. Thomas. Lincoln: Univ. of Nebraska Press, 1977.
Wirnt von Grafenberg. *Wigalois, Le Chevalier À La Roue.* Translated by Danielle Buschinger, Champion, 2004.
Wirnt von Grafenberg. *Wigalois.* Ed. Johannes Marie Neele Kapteyn. Translated by Sabine Seelbach and Ulrich Seelbach. 2nd ed., Berlin; Boston: De Gruyter, 2014.
Wolfram von Eschenbach. *Parzival.* Ed. Karl Lachmann, vol. 1. Revised and translated by Dieter Kühn. Frankfurt am Main: Deutscher Klassiker Verlag, 1994.

www.ingramcontent.com/pod-product-compliance
Lightning Source LLC
Chambersburg PA
CBHW070239240426
43673CB00044B/1856